Language Skill

Written by William Edmond

Published by Scholastic Publications Ltd,
Villiers House, Clarendon Avenue,
Leamington Spa, Warwickshire CV32 5PR

Written by William Edmonds
Edited by Janet Fisher
Sub-edited by Juliet Gladston
Illustrations by Bernie Williams
Front and back covers designed by
Keith Martin
Photograph by Martyn Chillmaid
Artwork by Steve Williams Design,
Leicester

Printed in Great Britain by Loxley Brothers
Ltd, Sheffield

British Library Cataloguing in Publication Data
A catalogue record for this book is
available from the British Library.

ISBN 0 590 53040 2

Contents

INTRODUCTION 4

BUILDING WORDS 6

Introducing the concept 8
Wonderful words 8
First words 9
Investigating words 10
Letter characteristics 11
Special letter days 11
Alphabet ordering 12
Vowel colours 12
Substitution word makers 14
Beginning pairs 15
Directing p's and q's 16
Consonant skeletons 17
'A' words 18
Combinations 19
Words within words 19
Plentiful plurals 20
Weather compounds 21
Run-ups 22
Suffixing 23
Goodness graciousness 24
Prefixing 25
Syllable rhythms 26
'Catching on' spelling techniques 27
Snap shots 27
Oddballs 28
Look! Write! Write! Write! Right? 29
Which witch is which? 30
Hard spots 31

WORKING WORDS 32

Introducing the parts of speech 34
Dictionary detectives 34
Word tickets 35
Highlighting 36
Cloze procedure 36
Naming (nouns) 37
Labelling 37
Name plates 38
Name captions 39
Name games 40
Going places 42
People and places 43
A to Z guides 44
Evocation 45
Name books 47
Indexing 46

Referring (pronouns) 48
The great I am 48
Guess who's who? 49
Demonstrating this and that 50
What is *it*? 51
Naming no names 52
Us and them 52
Confronting contractions 53
Describing (adjectives) 54
Varieties 54
A sea of faces 55
Adjective riddles 56
In one word 56
Wanted 57
Embroidering 58
Good alternatives 59
Aspirations 60
Specifying (articles) 61
Definitely or indefinitely? 61
Reacting (verbs) 62
Cat and mouse 62
Using initiative 63
Action stations 64
Behaviour 65
All go! 66
Qualifying (adverbs) 67
How it's done 67
Maybe sometimes always never 68
Shades of grey 69
Absolutely amazing reviews 70
Especially, really, actually 71
Directing (prepositions) 72
Positioning words 72
Missing! 73
Getting lost 74
Which way? 75
Extending (conjunctions) 76
Again and again and again... 76
Food combinations 76
One sentence stories 77

CONSTRUCTING SENTENCES 79
The sentence workshop 80
Exclamations 82
Sounding off 82
Oh no! 83
Commands 84
At the double 84
Orders of the day 85
Statements 86
Captivating captions 86
Floating thoughts 87
Definitions 88
Who did what? 89
Idle thoughts 90
Fact and fancy 91
Questions 92
Wondering why 92
Interviewing 93
Raising questions 94
Testing out 95
Quizzes 96
Explanations 97
Telling tales 97
If and when 98
Excuses excuses 99
Reporting 100
Opening shots 101
Story 'blurbs' 101
Getting the gist 102
Punctuation and capitalisation 103
Punctuation fireworks 103
Capital capitals 104
Making the point 105
Editing out *'and'* 106
Snatching conversations 107
Rounding up thoughts 108
Putting a stop to it 109

REPRODUCIBLE MATERIAL 110

INDEX OF SKILLS 127

REFERENCES 128

Introduction

Language is arguably the most precious of all human resources. It's a gift which is unique to our species; a gift which enables thinking, communication and all consciousness. The use of language, particularly in the form of speech, is a human facility which is almost impossible to suppress – try keeping any child quiet for a significant period of time! The quality of its use is crucial to the quality of living. It's a natural and very vital skill.

A key part of growing up and becoming a full social being is learning to be a skilful language user. This means adapting to and mastering particular linguistic conventions, knowing what they are, how they work and how to exploit them to advantage. It means getting to grips with the basic structures of language and learning to use them with maximum ease, effect and eloquence.

Much of the groundwork of language skill is accomplished well before most children start school. Young children invariably first learn to speak without anyone telling them how to. Spurred on by strong natural urges to make sense of their surroundings and to communicate with those around them, they discover for themselves a considerable knowledge about how language works and what it can do. Coming to school means a consolidation of this emergent expertise. It also means the introduction of a major new dimension: the issue of literacy and its standardised form.

This book deals with language skill as we meet it during the years of primary education. It naturally takes into account the major four spheres of language – listening, talking, reading and writing – recognising that these are all closely related. Most of the activities are designed to give children practice in developing skill in each of these areas, but it will be found that in the majority of cases there is an emphasis on an eventual written product. However, when the need for writing materials is stated, this should not be taken as compulsory. A word processor is a desirable extra tool and can be used effectively, sometimes extra effectively, in carrying out many of the activities.

The book makes no apology for bringing the notion of 'grammar' to the forefront. This is a good general descriptive term for the structural organisation of language. It is something which we all naturally generate for ourselves from our earliest speech. A large proportion of the activities are therefore based on harnessing and developing natural creative urges which further particular grammatical competences. In the process, an understanding and knowledge of the linguistic elements involved is specifically promoted. The activities also happen to take into account many of the special needs of pupils who are learning English as a second language and who are particularly helped by having structural frameworks to key in to.

The activity ideas are founded on the assumption that language acquisition is naturally an enjoyable and rewarding experience. Through the development of language skill our expressive powers are refined and each person finds his or her distinctive voice. This involves precision and also the honing of poetic sensitivity and style. In this way, our personalities grow and flower.

What are the essential elements of language skill? For the purposes of primary education and of this book we shall deal with them in three broad areas: *building words, working words, constructing sentences.*

ACTIVITY SELECTION

It is not the intention to provide a comprehensive curricular programme in this book. Language skill obviously extends much further than this book can allow for. Instead, a broad selection of ideas is provided which can be selected from, used, or adapted to fit particular needs and situations. Each activity is generally targeted for a particular age range, but this need not be adhered to too strictly. Often the basic principles of an activity will apply to other ages with a little adaptation. Indeed, the follow-up suggestions often indicate how this can be done.

It will also be seen that a large majority of the activities allow for a considerable flexibility in group sizes, whether the children are working individually, in pairs or in any other way.

Finally, there is a special index provided at the end of the book which lists all the linguistic skill elements and indicates in which activities you can find them.

It will be seen that many of these elements reappear in different places and across all three chapters.

Building words

What are words made of? This question (which prompts the first two activities in this section) is not easy to answer but it points to the dilemma concerning how we plunge into the process of word making. Which comes first, the meanings or the ways they are represented by sounds or marks? Or to be more specific, do we learn letters or whole words first when we start to read and write? Can we really separate handwriting and spelling skills?

Fortunately, recent research and successful practice relating to the notion of 'emergent language skill' has demonstrated the rewarding bandwagon effect of going straight into the 'whole processes' of reading and writing right from the start and harnessing the strong natural urge always to be creating meaning. The activities in this first section therefore attempt to engage the enthusiastic motivation of the children with the basic techniques of word making – in writing especially. They are concerned essentially with the combined processes of handwriting (skilled letter formation) and spelling (skilled letter selection). So that both processes can be mutually self-supporting – fluency is of the essence. So, too, is personal relevance.

This chapter begins with two sections of introductory activities which deal with the general composition of words. There then follows a selection of ideas which focus on particular features of individual letters. These are followed by a few suggestions for looking at ways of combining word parts. The chapter concludes with some ideas for 'catching on' spelling techniques.

Introducing the concept

Wonderful words

Objective

To draw attention to the wonder of words and their make-up.

Age range

Five to seven.

Group size

Groups of six.

What you need

Items containing words which can either be read or listened to, for instance, story tapes, a variety of books including picture dictionaries, objects with labels, felt-tipped pens, pencils, sheets of white paper, sugar paper, adhesive.

What to do

Show the children some of the different objects that you have collected and let them hear part of a story tape. Explain that all these items have words on them and then ask them what they think words are made of. Steer the discussion so that the children begin to think about what marks are used to make letters and what voice noises make sound. Talk about how wonderful words are, how they come in all sorts of shapes, sizes and sounds. Ask the children how many different words they think there might be and explain that they come in different languages too. Ask the children to think about and then say what their most

favourite or most wonderful words are. Discuss with the children the reasons for their choices.

Now ask the children to make a presentation of their wonderful words. Ask them to write them out in large decorated letters and help them to mount their words to make a display.

Follow-up

- Invite the children to make wonderful words which fall into different categories, such as, wonderful sounding words, wonderful looking words, wonderful meaning words, exciting words, fascinating words, extremely useful words, and so on.
- Encourage the children to write lists of 'words I know' (or 'know how to write') off the top of their heads.

First words

Objective
To focus on words which have a prime significance during the early stages of learning to talk and learning to read and write.

Age range
Five to seven.

Group size
Various.

What you need
Pencils, felt-tipped pens, white paper.

What to do
This activity is organised in three parts, and you may choose to do one or all of them.

The first part involves a discussion with the children about what they think might have been their very first spoken words. If they don't know, perhaps they have observed younger members of their family learning to talk. Ask the children to write out the words and make up a collective classroom poster entitled 'First words'.

The second part, which is best carried out during the first two weeks after children start school, is essentially a discussion about which written words the children know best and think are the best words to learn. Encourage the children to create a poster advertising 'Our first words at school'.

Thirdly, you can draw special attention to words which most commonly start sentences in the classroom or at home. Many of these are likely to be names or words like 'Miss', 'Mum', 'Dad', 'I', 'Please' (possibly) or words like 'Look', 'Can', 'Wait', and so on. For each of these starter words, ask the children which other words most often seem to follow it, for instance:

- 'Miss, can I go to the toilet please?'
- 'Miss, Andrew is pinching me.'
- 'Miss, when is it dinner?'
- 'Miss, what can I do now?'

Encourage the children to write out such common utterances beginning with the same starting word, as if they were short poems.

Investigating words

Objective

To investigate the nature and composition of words. The objective of this activity is similar to 'Wonderful Words', but is designed for older children.

Age range

Seven to ten.

Group size

Any.

What you need

An assortment of fiction and non-fiction books, dictionaries, newspapers and magazines, reference books on 'words', felt-tipped pens, white paper.

What to do

Start the investigation with a general class discussion arising from some of the following questions:

- What are words?
- What are they made up of?
- What different kinds of words are there?
- About how many different words do you think you know?
- About how many different words do you think there are?
- Which are easy words to spell?
- Which are difficult words to spell?
- Why can spelling sometimes be so tricky?
- What are your favourite and most used words?
- What are 'good' and 'bad' words?
- Which words from different languages do the children know?

Guide the discussion into more specific investigatory or speculative activities. For example:

- Ask the children to make lists of different kinds of words using a range of adjectives, for instance, good words, long words, difficult words, funny words and beautiful words.
- Invite the children to define what words are or what they can do. For instance: 'They help us to make friends'; 'They let us have thoughts'; 'They sit on paper'; 'They float across a room'; 'They are magic' and so on.
- Make a list of easy words to spell and then some more difficult words. Discuss and indicate to the children the specific difficulties of the more problematical words. Also discuss with them which ways best help to learn spellings.
- Ask the children to make posters or wall displays of a selection of words from different languages which some of the children know.
- Let the children cut out a number of newspaper headlines. Discuss with them their style and composition, and ask them to look for words which are most frequently used (these are usually words designed to have special impact). Ask the children to cut up the headlines to separate the words and then make up some fun alternative headlines.
- Invite the children to compare the quantities of words in different dictionaries and different spell-check computer programs. Let them estimate the number of words they know.

Letter characteristics

Special letter days

Objective
To create special days when individual letters are singled out for particular attention, emphasising their key value as initial letters.

Age range
Five to six.

Group size
The whole class and small groups.

What you need
Collections of objects relevant to the chosen letter, labels, a display area, story books, picture dictionaries, pencils, felt-tipped pens, paper, scrap materials, adhesive.

What to do
The day before your chosen letter day, ask the children to bring in an object or a picture of something whose name begins with the special letter. On the day, let the children help to make a display of these items (which can also be labelled) in a corner of the classroom. Other items which they find in the classroom can also be added. During the day, you can carry out a number of other activities with the children, such as:

- giving badges, special honours and privileges to any children whose first names begin with this letter;
- doing some relevant letter formation practice;
- compiling lists of words beginning with this letter;
- composing alliterative jingles;
- collecting together and reading books which have titles or important characters beginning with this letter;
- making pictures and models to add to the display area;
- inviting visitors to the class whose names begin with the letter;
- going on a ramble to look out for relevant items.

Follow-up
With the children's help, make up a classroom alphabet, for example:

- A is for Andrew, alphabet and **and**.
- B is for boys, books and badges.
- C is for Christine, coats, chairs and caterpillars.

Let the children compile a class book and/or make an assembly presentation with it.

- Draw the children's attention to phonetic anomalies, such as knees, knights, gnats, photos, cities, sugar, pterodactyls, and so on.

Alphabet ordering

Objective
To promote complete familiarity with alphabetical sequencing.

Age range
Five upwards.

Group size
Any.

What you need
Alphabet books, alphabet picture cards and charts.

What to do
Explain to the children that the main part of this activity involves setting out pictorial alphabet cards into alphabetical order on a shelf or ledge. Every day, ask a different pair of children to do this task. To help them, let the children sort the cards into smaller groupings, such as abcd, efg, hijk, lmn, opq, rst, uvw, xyz. Play games with the children by asking them to spot missing letters or jumbled pairs of letters.

Follow-up
- From time to time ask the children to make new cards for particular letters.
- Encourage the children to make up their own alphabetical registers of toy names for role playing.
- Show the children how to make their own alphabetically ordered spelling books.

Vowel colours

Objective
To draw attention to the five vowels and their distinctive sounds by associating them with colours.

Age range
Five to ten. Older children will find more challenge in some of the follow-up activities.

Group size
Any.

What you need
Pencils, felt-tipped pens, large sheets of paper, scissors.

What to do

Write on a board five different one-syllable words, each with a different single middle vowel, for example, 'catch', 'when', 'sit', 'stop' and 'sun'.

Point out that each word has a distinctly different main sound given to it by its vowel. Suggest that each of these vowel sounds could have its own colour and ask the children for ideas about what colour best suits each vowel.

When a colour code has been agreed, ask the children to suggest other words which might belong to each colour.

Then ask them to draw and colour five large balloons on which they can write a selection of appropriate words.

Follow-up

- Ask the children to use the different colours to colour in the vowels on a piece of enlarged printed text. They can then investigate how much of each colour there is and illustrate the relative colour proportions with a histogram.
- Draw the children's attention to words which have a silent final 'e' and give a few examples like hate, wine, hope and cute. What happens to each word if the 'e' is deleted? Can the children find more words where this happens?

Let the children decide what should be done about colouring in the vowel sounds in such cases.

- Ask the children to solve the following problems:

When can an 'e' become a 'u' colour? (few, knew...)
When can an 'e' and an 'i' become an 'a' colour? (eight)
When can an 'o' become a 'u' colour? (one, to...)
When can an 'i' become an 'e' colour? (ski)

- Discuss with the children the fact that each vowel actually has a range of different 'sound colours' according to its context within a word. Explain that this range of colours is a special feature (and problem) of the English language.

Help the children to make up colour charts to illustrate each different vowel sound, including digraphs like 'ee', 'ie'. The chart should indicate how different vowels can sometimes end up making the same sound colour.

- Invite the children to make up booklets or charts with each page or section having a collection of rhyming words and its own distinctive colour.

titution word makers

e
nstrate how new words are made by simply
ng one letter.

Age range
Five to seven.

Group size
Up to six.

What you need
A word maker – a vertical strip with the letters b, c, ch, f, gn, h, m, p, r, s, th, and wh and a main card with the letters at (see illustration), squares of thinnish card (about 10cm x 10cm) – preferably with two 1cm slits already cut in the right place, thin strips of card (about 1cm wide and 20cm long), pencils.

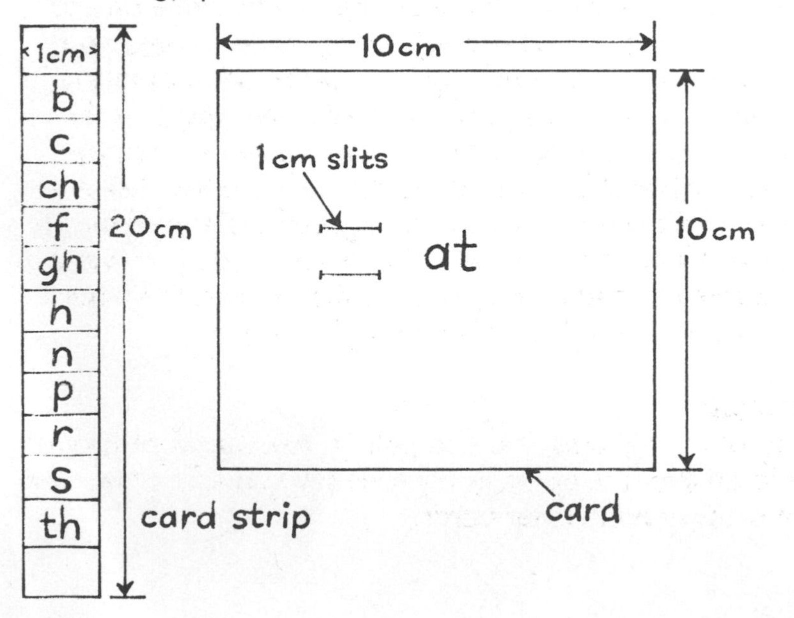

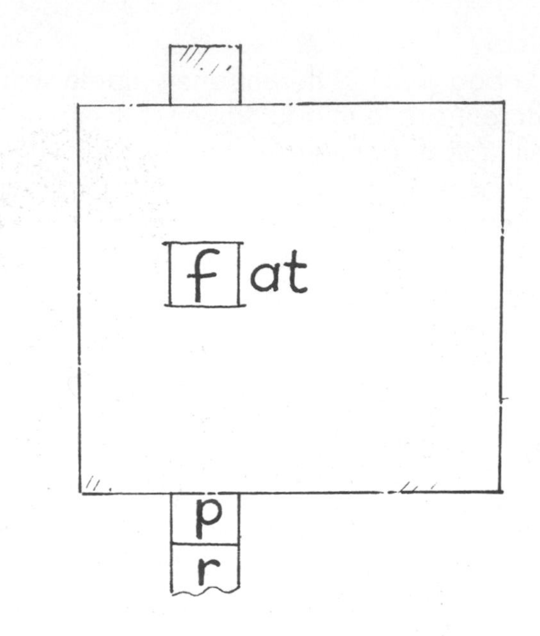

What to do
Show the children how a ready-made word maker works and ask them to read the different words which are made when the initial letter(s) is changed.

Give the children the materials to make their own word makers with simple word endings like -in, -en, -an, -ad, -end, -ent, -op, -it, -ank, -on, -ome, -oot, -ight, -ought, and so on. Make allowances for a fair amount of trial and error in the making and spacing of the strips. When completed, ask the children to swap their strips with others to see how many different words with a similar pattern they can make. They will no doubt make a few nonsense words too!

Follow-up
• Draw the children's attention to rhyming words which may be created with the word maker. Can the children make these rhyming words into a short verse?

Beginning pairs

Objective
To focus on the first two letters in the building of words.

Age range
Six to eight.

Group size
Groups of four.

What you need
Photocopiable pages 111 and 112, a dictionary.

What to do
Cut out several sets of the alphabet cards from photocopiable pages 111 and 112 and share or deal them out so that each player has ten cards. Leave the rest face down in the middle of the table. Ask the first player to turn over one of these cards. She must then try to place one of her own letters after it to make the beginning of any word she chooses. If it is agreed that this combination of letters begins a word, then the player can keep her 'pair'. If the player makes a mistake or fails to make a workable pair then the card must be returned to the centre pack. Ask the players to follow each other in an agreed order and the first child to have used all his original ten cards (and so to have made ten 'beginning pairs') is the winner. Point out that no word should be called more than once.

Follow-up
Instead of taking turns and competing, ask a pair or group of children to make up as many 'opening pairs' as they can out of a selection of letter cards.

Directing p's and q's

Objective
To help with the correct directioning of the letters p, q, d and b.

Age range
Six to nine.

Group size
Small groups.

What you need
Scissors, adhesive, coloured paper, letter templates (for younger children), pencils, a large sheet of paper.

What to do
First provide or ask the children to cut out some 'p' shapes. When a fair number have been produced, scatter them randomly on a table or large piece of paper. Ask the children to look from one side of the table and identify any letters which they see. Then ask them to try again from the opposite side of the table. You can also experiment with flipping the shapes over.

When the children have seen how the same shape can lead to the four different letters and how the letters can easily be changed, ask them to make them into a picture. They can either stick the letters on the sheet of paper in a random pattern or else they can stick them in different letter groups in four sections of the paper.

Follow-up
• Let the children use mirrors to look at their pictures.
• Ask the children to make collections of words starting with b, d, p or q. They can write these on tickets or wall charts and play sorting or posting games with the tickets.
• Let the children practise writing lots of short (three letter) words beginning with 'p' (lower case) as fast and fluently as possible: for example pen, pot, pat, pit, pod and so on. Then let them practise writing lots of 'qu's – cursively or as near to cursively as possible. They can also write some short 'qu' words. Similar fast practices can be done with 'b' and 'd' words.

Consonant skeletons

Objective
To draw attention to the role of consonants in making up word skeletons.

Age range
Six to nine.

Group size
Any.

What you need
Books about animals, dictionaries, pencils and paper.

What to do
Write a few examples of animal word skeletons (animal names with spaces left instead of vowels) on the board. For example, l _ _ n, l _ _ p _ rd, sn _ k _, h _ pp _ p _ t _ m _ s, m _ _ s _.

Ask the children to say what letters should occupy each space. Discuss with them what kind of letters these are. Suggest that consonants make up the hard 'skeleton' part of words while vowels can be thought of as the fleshy parts. Discuss also the special role of the letter 'y' which can sometimes take on a vowel function as in 'fly'.

When this distinction between vowels and consonants is understood and appreciated, invite the children to make their own lists of animal word skeletons with the help of some animal reference books. The children can then swap their word skeletons and complete the puzzles.

Follow-up
The children can practise deciphering and composing sentences written in consonant shorthand – where all the vowels have been removed for example:
Tdy w r gng t d sme shrthnd.
Th bg dg rn wy dwn th rd.
Cn y wrt lk ths?

'A' words

Objectives
To examine which letters normally follow each other and to discover the only letter of the alphabet which can be followed by all the others, including itself.

Age range
Eight to ten.

Group size
Pairs or small groups.

What you need
Dictionaries, pencils, paper.

What to do
Challenge the children to find the only letter in the alphabet which can be followed by all of the others including itself – as this happens to be the first letter of the alphabet it should be found fairly quickly! Once they have discovered the letter ask them to make an 'A Team' – a list of 26 words beginning with 'a' but followed by a different letter each time. (Aa and Ao are the only ones likely to cause any problem so, if necessary, you could prompt the children with aardvark and aorta).

Follow-up
- Invite the children to find the 'B Team'. (B has only eight different following letters).
- Ask the children to find the only letter which can only be followed by one other ('q' – except in a few Arabic names) and the only letters which can then follow 'qu'.

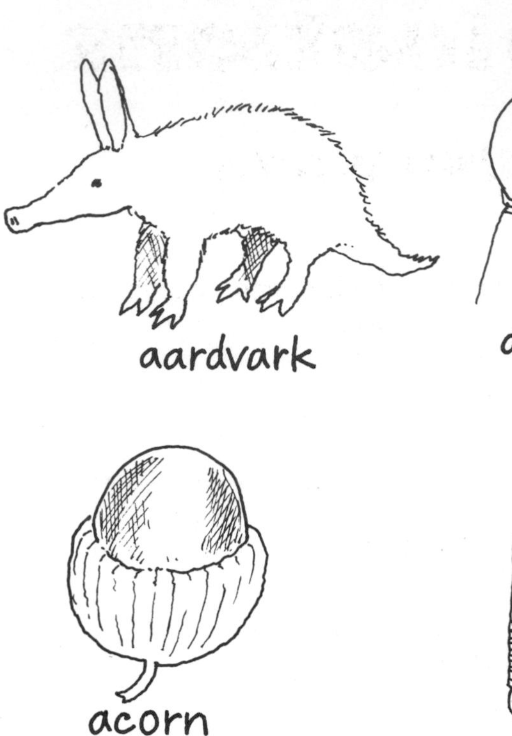

Combinations

Words within words

Objective
To build up spelling confidence by encouraging the recognition of words within words.

Age range
Five to eight.

Group size
Small groups or the whole class.

What you need
Pencils, paper, felt-tipped pens.

What to do
Write on the board some children's names which have recognisable smaller words within their spellings, for instance Jane, Christopher, Catherine and Peter. Ask the children to spot which name contains the particular smaller words: cat, is, pet, her and the. Ask them to see what other words they can find and how many different words are inside each name. Suggest that they write all of the 'inside' words under each of the names. Look with the children at a few other examples and explain to them that not all names have other words in their spellings.

Ask the children to examine their own names (perhaps giving them the option of looking at either their first name or last name, or even the names of other members of their family). Invite them to draw pictures of themselves or of someone else, putting the name underneath and any smaller 'inside words' on the body. Suggest that they draw pictures within pictures, such as a picture of a top within a picture of Christopher.

Follow-up
- The same principle can be applied to any words; encourage the children to try finding other 'words within words' using a short piece of text. Challenge them to see how many they can find.
- Certain words are particularly rich with 'insiders' – information (10), knowledge (7), grandfather (8), teacher (5), scared (7), scapegoat (9), shallow (7). Challenge the children to find all the 'insiders' of words like these and to find other words which are equally as rich.

Plentiful plurals

Objective
To look at and collect a wide variety of nouns in a plural form.

Age range
Six to nine.

Group size
Individuals or pairs.

What you need
Paper (including large sheets), pencils, felt-tipped pens, dictionaries.

What to do
On the board, draw a large shape to represent an island. Tell the children that this is the 'Land of Plenty' where there is lots and lots of everything. Ask the children to think of things which may be on the island and draw these suggestions on the island, for example pin-sized people, money, trees, sheep, wolves, mice, mountains, cars, lorries, cacti, and so on. As each new group is added, write the plural names around the edge of the island, grouping the names according to types of plurals, for instance 's' words, 'es' words, 'ies' words, words without a final 's' and words that don't change. The children should begin to see that the objective is to draw their attention to the unusual plural words as well as common ones.

When the children understand this general objective, ask them to make their own 'Lands of Plenty' in the same way.

Weather compounds

Objective
To show how compound nouns can be made by adding further nouns to the principal weather elements: rain, sun, snow and wind.

Age range
Six to nine.

Group size
Any.

What you need
Large sheets of paper, pencils, pens, rulers.

What to do
Write out rain, sun, snow and wind as headings across the top of the board. Explain to the children what is meant by a compound noun and then ask them to think of any compound nouns which begin with one of the words on the board. Write the second parts of these compound nouns in a random order and in a line at the bottom of the board, for example: shine, rise, glasses, screen, light, fall, dial, bow, flower, day, break, drop, burn, swept, set, flake, mill, man, coat, ball, storm and so on. Draw dotted lines to link each element to the words with which it can be combined. Finally, count and record the total number of lines or compound words that have been created.

When the children have grasped the idea, give them each a large sheet of paper and ask them to create their own compound nouns in the same way.

Run-ups

Objective
To practise creating words by having 'run-ups' to them.

Age range
Six to nine.

Group size
Any.

What you need
No special requirements.

What to do
Start by explaining to the children that they are going to play a word game. You should then think of a word and say it three times. After saying it three times you must add to the word to make a new word, for example:

- bet, bet, bet, better;
- bat, bat, bat, batter;
- mis, mis, mis, mischief;
- slip, slip, slip, slipper;
- slipper, slipper, slipper, slippery.

After you have given them a few examples, let the children call out any final new words. Follow this by asking a child to make the start word for another child to finish. Encourage the children to keep to a rhythmic pattern each time. See how many children can come up with a final word.

Follow-up
For some writing practice, give the children a range of starters and ask them to write three 'run ups' and a final word; for example:

- go, go, go, good;
- good, good, good, goodness;
- ban . . . ;
- to . . . ;
- the . . . .

Suffixing

Objectives
To practise adding the suffix '-ing' to root verb forms and to develop writing fluency by making up lines which play upon the notion of gathering momentum.

Age range
Six to eight.

Group size
Any.

What you need
Paper, pencils.

What to do
With the class, make a collection of verbs (action or being words or even 'command words'). Write them on the board in their root form and, without explaining why, keep them in three groups:

- those where '-ing' can be added without any change – for example, go, look, walk, jump, add, wait, eat, sleep, flow;
- those requiring the deletion of a final 'e' before adding '-ing', for example, come, have, make, leave, write, hope;
- those requiring the doubling of a final consonant before adding 'ing' for example, stop, run, hop, skip, swim.

Demonstrate with an example from the first group how the suffix '-ing' can be added and how this participle can now be written repeatedly to create a sense of momentum which can end with an abrupt conclusion. For example:

- going going going going going going GONE!
- looking looking looking looking looking FOUND IT!

Running, running, running!

- walking walking walking walking walking OW! MY FEET ACHE!

Now invite the children to make up and write some lines of their own, using only the words from the first group to start with.

Follow-up
- Explain to the children what has to be done with the other two groups of words and ask them to make similar jokey lines.
- Invite the children to arrange or plan the lines so that they make a kind of story, like the one below.

Going, going, going, go!
Walking,walking, walking, walk!
Running, running, running, run!
Racing, racing, racing, race!
Hurrying, hurrying, hurrying, hurry!
Arriving, arriving, arriving, arrived!

Goodness graciousness

Objective

To use the suffix '-ness' to make nouns out of adjectives.

Age range

Seven to ten.

Group size

Any.

What you need

Pencils, paper, felt-tipped pens.

What to do

Ask the children to help you write a selection of adjectives on the board. If a sentence-making workshop (see page 80) is in operation, the children can use the appropriate box to supply some of the words. Invite the children to see what happens if the suffix '-ness' is added to some of these adjectives. Draw their attention to adjectives ending with 'y' and to how this letter changes to an 'i', when adding '-ness' – happy/happiness. Circle or underline the new nouns that work successfully. Ask the children to write down and make up a few '-ness' nouns of their own. They could call the page something like 'Goodness graciousness' and decorate it appropriately.

Follow-up

In a similar way, ask the children to make a collection of words using the suffix '-ful' to turn nouns into adjectives, drawing their attention to the changed spelling of 'full' to 'ful'.

Prefixing

Objectives

To draw attention to common prefixes and to make groupings of words which use particular ones.

Age range

Seven to eleven.

Group size

Any.

What you need

Pencils, paper, dictionaries.

What to do

Draw a square on the board and write the words 'over', 'in', 'out' and 'under' outside the four sides. Inside the square (which should have enough space for up to 30 words), write down some words which could be combined with one or more of the prefixes. Ask the children to see if they can suggest some other examples to go in the middle of the square. After a few examples have been contributed, delete the centre prefixed words and ask the children to make their own squares, on pieces of paper, putting as many words as they can into the middle. Encourage them to use dictionaries.

Possible centre words include: number, coat, take, look, spire, put, form, line, ground, standing, law, side, skirts, flow, loyed, rage, growth, done, sleep, tend, spoken, accurate, smart, deed, ward or crease.

Follow-up

- Invite the children to make miniature anthology booklets of prefixtures. Encourage them to use snappy titles for the various prefix word groupings, for example, 'In words', 'Undone words', 'Out words', 'With-it words', and so on.
- Encourage the children to play on the 'eggs' punning of the 'ex' prefix and make an 'eggshibition' of decorated eggs with labels such as 'eggsecutioner', 'eggspert', 'eggsplorer', and so on.
- Ask the children to use prefixes for practice 'run-ups' as on page 23.

Syllable rhythms

Objective
To draw attention to the syllables in words and their distinctive beats by using words of different numbers and emphases of syllables to make rhythm patterns.

Age range
Seven to eleven.

Group size
The whole class divided into three or four groups.

What you need
Drums or any improvised percussion instruments.

What you do
Make sure that the children know what syllables are. Ask the children to go to one of three or possibly four corners of the room, according to how many syllables they have in their first names. Then tell the groups to arrange themselves in a line so that you can easily point to each child. Ask them to call out their names as you point to them (maybe with a conductor's baton). At first, point in a steady rhythm at each member of the different groups and then start making rhythmic patterns by alternating between groups.

Follow this by directing individuals or whole groups to make similar rhythms by clapping and/or using percussion instruments. Ask the children to alternate the beats with each name calling so that they build up a rhythmic sound poem.

Discuss with the children the notion of the different accents on syllables. Help them to prepare for a performance in front of an audience.

Follow-up
- Invite the children to make sound poems out of other names or words, for example animals, foods, breakfast cereals, places, football teams, and dinosaurs, encouraging plenty of rhythmic repetition. Help them to elaborate the sounds with a musical accompaniment of guitars. Encourage small groups to make their own compositions.
- Ask the children to make lists of names with different numbers of syllables. Which words have the largest number of syllables?
- Investigate with the children the relative frequency of one-syllable, two-syllable, three–syllable and four-syllable words by checking through a small sample of text. Let the children record their findings on a histogram graph.
- Let the children write a short story or poem in words of only one syllable (which might well use shorthand or abbreviated words), for instance, 'Why did the cat sit on the mat?'

'Catching on' spelling techniques

Snap shots

Objectives
To introduce the idea of visual memory being a key part of spelling skills and to practise 'photographic' focusing and recall techniques with simple 'spelling cameras'.

Age range
Six to ten.

Groups size
Any.

What you need
Photocopiable page 113, a sample 'spelling camera' ready made-up, scissors, pens, pencils, paper.

What to do
Show a sample 'spelling camera' to the children and demonstrate how it can be placed on a page of writing so as to frame an individual word. A snap shot of this word can then be taken in three stages. First, they should focus carefully on the whole word. Second, they should fix its image into their minds and push the shutter down. Third, they should make a print by writing out the word from memory on the special printing paper.

Help the children to make their own spelling cameras using photocopiable page 113. Cameras of different sized lens holes can be made so as to be able to deal with different sized print, varying word lengths and also distant viewing of words on a board.

Ask the children to practise putting their spelling cameras to use either with specially selected spellings or allowing them to select their own words from a piece of text (such as photocopiable page 115) or book.

All prints should be checked for quality control.

Follow-up
- Let the children experiment to see how long the photographic memory can be made to last. This can be done by extending the period between snapping and developing to half an hour or even up to several days.
- For distant snap shots, encourage the children to make box cameras.

Oddballs

Objective
To draw special attention to 'oddball' spellings.

Age range
Six to eleven.

Group size
Individuals.

What you need
Coloured paper, different sized coins or larger round objects such as circle templates, felt-tipped pens, scissors.

What to do
Discuss with the children the idea of 'oddball' words – ones which flout phonetic conversation, catch you by surprise, or commonly trip you up. Let the children attempt to write some of these on the board, using a trial and error process. Put circles around the correct versions, making them look like different sized balls. Then ask the children to make their own selection of oddballs. Let them do this on paper of different colours and then cut them out and mount them for a wall display.

The following are examples of such words: Wednesday, ceiling, because, colonel, know, there, one, two, eight, Christmas, station, rhubarb, bomb and tongue.

Follow-up
- Make oddball shapes with blank letter spaces inside. Write below them clues about the words that the children should fill in.
- Throw a ball to a child and if he catches it he has to call out the spelling of an oddball word. Give five points for a catch and five more if a correct spelling is made. It is probably best if you suggest the oddball word or if a child reads one from a ready prepared list.

Look! Write! Write! Write! Right?

Objective
To practise another version of the spelling technique of 'Look, cover, write, check' which also helps to develop writing fluency by requiring repeated attempts.

Age range
Seven to eleven.

Group size
Individuals.

What you need
Photocopiable page 114.

What to do
Give each child a copy of photocopiable page 114 and show them how to fold it in thirds to make a zigzag spelling processor. Explain that in the 'look' column the child must carefully copy a problematical word of her choice, or a word which she has been directed to learn.

After attempting to put this word into photographic memory, ask the child to turn the page and print or write out the word again in the 'write' column. Explain that by folding the zigzag machine twice more the 'write again' and the 'and again' columns will be reached and she should write out the word again there. Ask the child to check the third attempt against the original version. The system is seen to be working if most of the attempts are correct.

The processor allows for a selection of words to be learned and practised in this way. This can be a good general exercise and it can also be helpful when preparing for a test.

Follow-up
- Set timed targets for the exercise.
- Apply the same principles to repeated tries on a word processor with the screen turned away from the keyboard while the children type the word.

Which witch is which?

Objectives
To look at homophones and to make puzzle-type questions out of the confusions they can sometimes cause.

Age range
Six to eleven.

Group size
Start with the whole class or group and then go on to working individually or in pairs.

What you need
Dictionaries, photocopiable page 115, pencils, paper.

What to do
Begin by asking the children a few riddle-like questions based on homophones. For example:
- What is a plaice place? (Fish shop or the sea)
- What was the arc over the ark? (Rainbow)
- When is a bean been? (When it has been eaten)
- What makes a bough bow? (The wind or a person swinging on it)
- Where does meat meet? (At the butcher's)

After you have given and discussed a few examples like this, ask the children to identify the general principle from which these questions have been made, that is, the nature of homophones. Ask them to suggest a few others and to make up similar questions.

Invite the children to write out some homophone puzzles of their own. You could give them a photocopiable page 115 to help. They could try out their questions on another audience.

The ark under the arc.

Follow-up
- Encourage the children to write a nonsense story which deliberately uses as many misplaced homophones as possible. Let them swap their stories and ask their readers to spot how many homophones there are.
- Let the children compile an alphabet of homophone pairs (pears).
- If you have a word processing system with a spellcheck system, let the children test it by trying all sorts of misspellings which are close to homophones: plase playss playse plais pleys.

Hard spots

Objectives
To focus on and practise problematical letter patterns within spellings.

Age range
Seven to eleven.

Group size
Any.

What you need
Samples of normal text, preferably in fairly large print (see photocopiable page 116), pencils, paper.

What to do
Discuss with the children the problem of 'difficult bits' within spellings and how they can be dealt with. For example, words like Christmas can be abbreviated to Xmas, spaghetti can be abandoned for pasta or else fused handwriting can cover over difficulties. Give the children copies of some sample text and ask them to ring or highlight a selected number (say five) of tricky three- letter sequences.

Then ask them to practise writing those 'hard spots' as repeated letter patterns, using cursive or as near cursive script as possible. For each letter pattern, see if they can find and list other words using it.

Follow-up
- Ask the children to focus on three-consonant clusters.
- Let them concentrate on vowel liaisons (twos and threes).
- Present an already spotted (blotted out) text to be used for cloze procedure practice (see the bottom of photocopiable page 116).

Working words

These activities focus on the functioning of 'parts of speech' – the grammatical roles which words take on when they are strung together to make meaningful utterances. We generally consider these to comprise the following: nouns, pronouns, adjectives, verbs, adverbs, interjections, articles, prepositions and conjunctions. This is the standard word categorisation which is recognised in most dictionaries. It offers a useful way of describing how we manipulate words to make good sense and it provides a particularly helpful framework for the translation and learning of other languages. But it is not by any means a totally hard and fast rule-bound system – sometimes the precise role a word takes may be open to question. When applied prescriptively, it can quickly become a counter-productive drudgery, as so many of the more old fashioned books of 'English exercises' have testified.

The activities in this second chapter are designed to provide relevant contexts in which the different parts of speech can be made to demonstrate their particular functions in meaningful, stylish and rewarding ways. Nouns, pronouns, adjectives, articles, verbs, adverbs, prepositions and conjunctions are introduced in succession as categories of words, each with particular working roles to perform. Interjections make their point at the beginning of the third section.

Introducing the parts of speech

Dictionary detectives

Objective
To investigate grammatical terminology generally used in dictionaries.

Age range
Eight upwards.

Group size
Any.

What you need
Dictionaries.

What to do
Give out the dictionaries to the children and tell them that they are going to investigate how the words are labelled. Most dictionaries, including junior ones, list with each word its grammatical part of speech. This is usually noted as an abbreviation, for example *adj., v., adv., n., interj., pron., prep.,* and *art.*

Ask the children to carry out a survey to find a number of examples from each category, perhaps just keeping to those words beginning with the letter 'a'. Afterwards, you can discuss as a class their findings and try to identify features which typify each group.

Word tickets

Objective
To become familiar with grammatical categorisation of words.

Age range
Eight upwards.

Group size
Any.

What you need
Pencils, card tickets in eight different colours.

What to do
Ask the children to start making collections of single words – new words or ones they have difficulty spelling – on tickets of eight different colours. Tell them that each colour represents a different grammatical role, that is, noun, verb, adverb, pronoun, adjective, interjection, preposition and article. Encourage the children to store each colour of ticket in a separate labelled box and then use them as a spelling reference. The children should soon realise that many words can take on more than one role and thereby have multiple entries.

The children can gradually build up their collection of tickets in preparation for using them in the 'Sentence workshop' (see page 80).

Highlighting

Objective
To become familiar with grammatical categories of words.

Age range
Seven upwards.

Group size
Individuals.

What you need
Copies of printed text, coloured pencils or felt-tipped pens.

What to do
Give each child a copy of some printed text with relatively large letters (you could use the enlarging facility of a photocopier with some photocopiable text). Ask the children to read the text and highlight all the nouns in one colour, all the verbs in another colour, and so on. You will probably find it better to stick just to nouns, verbs and adjectives, and not necessarily on the same piece of text.

Cloze procedure

Objective
To use words appropriately.

Age range
Seven upwards.

Group size
Individuals.

What you need
Photocopiable page 117, pencils.

What to do
Give each child a copy of page 117. Ask the children to fill in the blanks with what they think might be suitable and/or entertaining words.

Naming (nouns)

Among the various parts of speech, nouns are by far the most abundant. There are far more nouns than all the other parts of speech put together. (Take a quick look at any page in a dictionary to see this for yourself.) Naming is one of the first and most basic forms of language use and it plays a key part in all early discovery. By giving correct names (or even inventing new ones) for any object, living thing, situation or branch of knowledge, we demonstrate expertise, good memory and powers of discernment.

Labelling

Objective
To enhance oral and written knowledge of noun vocabulary through the practice of labelling.

Age range
Five to seven.

Group size
Small groups.

What you need
A quantity of ticket-sized pieces of plain paper, Blu-Tack, pencils, a good picture dictionary or picture word book; for example: *Best Word Book Ever* by Richard Scarry (Hamlyn), *Spots Big Book of Words* by Eric Hill (Heinemann), *The Usborne Picture Dictionary, Puffin Picture Dictionary* by C. Berridge, *The Oxford ABC Picture Dictionary, 1000 Words and Pictures* (Ladybird).

What to do
Present the children with the challenge of naming as many objects and details of objects as they can see in a particular area of the classroom. Give each group several pieces of paper to use as labels and encourage them to try out their own spellings and free placing before fixing them in place.

Discuss and check with the children the accuracy of the words, their spellings and the neatness of the writing. Tell them to revise and re-label where necessary and then let them fix the labels in place.

Ask them to add a larger general label which describes what all the smaller labels are about, how many different names can be seen and, maybe, that such words are called nouns.

-up

ourage older children to label more obscure details (if objects are very small, they could use numbered spot els and a key to show which names go with each mber). Suggest that they even look for flaws and lemishes such as cracks, spots or cobwebs on the wall.

• Ask the children to apply the same procedure to a topic exhibition or an exhibition of models.

• Extend the labelling to include every part of the classroom so that the classroom itself resembles a section of a grand picture dictionary.

• Invite visitors to inspect and ask the children about the items which have been labelled.

• Help the children to distinguish between proper and common nouns by using different coloured labels.

Name plates

Objective
To practise recognising key written names to build up a sight vocabulary.

Age range
Five to six.

Group size
Any.

What you need
A set of name plates (in a variety of shapes and forms) for some of the principal objects and areas of the classroom.

What to do
Ask the children to take turns in setting out the labels each day in the right places. At first they could put them against matching cards. Alternatively, give each child one name plate to place. At a later date the labels could be made to include the names of all the children in the class. These can then be placed in the correct work draws or trays.

Name captions

Objective
To practise detailed naming by covering a picture with name captions.

Age range
Six to eight.

Group size
Individuals, pairs or small groups.

What you need
Magazine or newspaper pictures (a variety of portraits and general everyday scenes), pencils, self-adhesive labels, picture dictionaries, picture word books.

What to do
Start by looking together at some pages from a picture word book – where there are labelled pictures. Tell the children that they are going to put similar detailed captions on to some ordinary pictures which have been cut out from magazines and newspapers. To give them the idea, hold up one or two pictures and invite the children to name the details which they see and which could be labelled. Let the children choose pictures which they would like to label and invite them to put on as many name captions as they possibly can. They can either write the captions directly on to the picture (this is more immediate and less fussy) or on to labels which can then be stuck on to the picture.

Mount the captioned pictures and put them on a display board or combine them to make up picture word books.

Follow-up
- For younger or less confident children, provide a good range of ready-made self-adhesive labels for them to attach where appropriate.
- Let the children draw their own pictures to label, for instance, a fun fair, the seaside, a zoo, traffic, a playground, a classroom, a bedroom, toys and so on.
- Encourage the children to invent completely new names (from their own secret language) for common objects.
- Use the labelled pictures to play 'I spy' – type guessing games.

Name games

Objectives

To foster an awareness of nouns as a particular category of words and to distinguish between different kinds of nouns.

Age range

Six to nine.

Group size

Groups of six to ten.

What you need

No special requirements.

What to do

- Game 1 – Name chains

Decide on a particular grouping or linking of nouns, for instance, common nouns all beginning with the same letter, a list of proper nouns which each start with the last letter of the previous noun, anything currently visible, places, things that move and so on.

Ask each member of the group in turn to name an appropriate noun. If a child repeats a noun or gives a word which is not a noun, she has to drop out. The object is to see who can stay in the game the longest. It is advisable to set a time limit.

- Game 2 – Look, cover and recall

Ask the children to look at a detailed page in a word book or at a sizeable collection of objects and scrutinise every

detail. They should then close up the book or cover the objects and see how many of the names they can recall, either orally or in writing.

• Game 3 – Collective shopping

Start the children off by saying 'I went to the market and bought...' and adding an object. Ask each player in turn to recall and then add to the list a collective noun, for example:

'I went to the market and bought a bunch of bananas'.

'I went to the market and bought a bunch of bananas and a herd of cows'.

'I went to the market and bought a bunch of bananas, a herd of cows and an assortment of sweets'.

The player who can keep going the longest without any repetition or error is the winner.

• Game 4 – Guess what!

Invite a player or team to think of a relatively obscure noun. Explain that the rest of the children have to find out what the noun is by asking questions which can only be answered with yes or no. Give the questioners a limited number of questions (say 20) and if they can't guess the noun by then, the first player wins the round. The children could also play this game using proper nouns and the questions Guess who? or Guess where?

• Game 5 – Associations

Ask the players to call out, in turn, a different noun which can be associated in any way with the previous one that has been called. Encourage the children to call out the first word which comes to mind but remind them that only nouns are allowed. Using plurals helps to draw attention to the peculiar nature of plural nouns. For example: cats, fur, coats, rain, drops, puddles, muddles, messes, mice and cheese. Such word association can, of course, be worked upon afterwards and written up as short poems.

Going places

Objectives
To make and use a chart which shows the names of places within various distances of the school.

Age range
Five to nine.

Group size
Any.

What you need
Pencils, felt-tipped pens, large pieces of paper, scissors, adhesive, postcards.

What to do
With the help of suggestions and discussion with the children, construct a radial chart. This will have the school at the centre with arrows pointing away from it to the names of a variety of places which the children commonly visit. Try to relate the relative length of the arrows to the relative distance of the places from the school. When completed, display the chart as a spelling reference source. Encourage the children to illustrate it with postcards or drawings.

Let the children make their own versions of this chart, indicating places which are special to them.

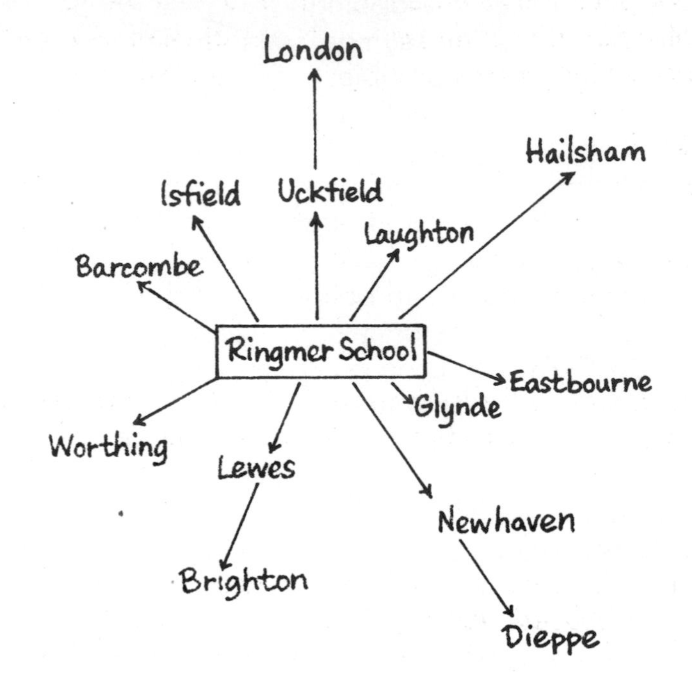

Follow-up
- After the main holidays, invite the children to make a similar chart to show all the different places which they visited during the holidays.
- Encourage the children to recognise local place names by setting up a postal sorting office. The children can then address envelopes or cards to be posted and sort them by place name into labelled pigeon holes.
- Jumble up the letters of familiar place names (and people's names too). Encourage the children to pick out the initial capital letter first and solve the anagrams. Here are some examples: rimBhaming, ermAcai, andStocl, noBghtri.

People and places

Objective

To draw attention to proper nouns and their initial capitalisation by making associations of particular people with particular places.

Age range

Eight to eleven.

Group size

Any.

What you need

Pencils, paper, atlases, television listings magazines or other magazines which contain plenty of names of celebrities.

What to do

On one side of the board write 'People' and on the other side write 'Places'. Ask the children to think of the names of some famous people and, in particular, try to elicit the names of people from a variety of different well-known places and countries, for example; sports, major political figures, pop and film stars, characters from television soaps, possibly even historical characters. Write some of these names on the 'people' side of the board. On the other side, with the help of children's suggestions, write some names of places and countries where these people live or come from. Also ask the children to name some more distant places where members of their families may live, and write these down too.

Now ask the children to write list-type compositions linking people and places. Suggest that they start with more famous people and places, then mention people they know and complete the list with themselves.

Maradona Lives in Argentina.
Nelson Mandela lives in Africa.
Imran Khan lives in Pakistan.
Queen Elizabeth lives in London.
My uncle Jim lives in Manchester.
My grandmother lives in Wales.
I live at 31 Terminus Street, Brighton.

Remind them about the use of initial capital letters for proper names and 'I'.

A to Z introductory guides

Objective
To become aware of principal names associated with particular subjects.

Age range
Seven to eleven.

Group size
Individuals or pairs.

What you need
A4 size paper, pencils, felt-tipped pens, a wide range of topic information books.

What to do
Tell the children that they are going to make introductory A to Z brochures about a range of interesting topics. Show them an example of a folded piece of A4 paper on which you have already started such a brochure.

Ask the children to find an information book about a subject which particularly interests them or which may be quite new to them. Encourage them to research the subject in the information books (making particular use of indexes) to compile an alphabetical list of salient aspects or details of their particular topic. Advise the children to space out the entries they make in the brochure. Also suggest that they do not write out the whole alphabet at the start as they may wish to leave out one or two letters. Encourage them to create neat little illustrations and a careful layout.

When the children have completed their guides, they can swap them with their friends and then display them.

Evocation

Objective
To make selections of single nouns which evoke the sensation of a particular experience or circumstance, for instance, the pleasure of a beautiful spring day.

Age range
Six to nine.

Group size
Any.

What you need
A special place away from the classroom, such as an attractive spot in a park on a beautiful day, a churchyard, a street corner or the school kitchens; paper, pencils, felt-tipped pens.

What to do
Remind the children of the main senses: seeing, hearing, smelling and feeling. Tell them that they are going to have an opportunity of using all these senses in a special place. Make a brief visit to this place and ask the children to make a note (literally or mentally) of every detail they observe with each different sense while on the visit. Insist on a period of silence to take in the background noises.

On returning to the classroom, ask the children (without further discussion) to copy or write out lists of the various sights, sounds, smells and feelings that they experienced or associate with this particular place. Explain to them that the lists need not only be of nouns, but can also include more descriptive noun phrases.

Later on let the children edit and adapt their lists and make up evocative one-word short line poems. The visual aspects of the visit will obviously lend themselves to illustration and other artwork.

Follow-up
• Rather than make individual recollections, let the children compile a collective list of recalled sensations.
• With the children, carry out a similar exercise but without moving from the classroom. To do this tell the children to simply imagine and then list all the sensations of a place where they long to be.

Indexing

Objectives

To complete indexes and to learn about selecting principal content nouns and alphabetical ordering.

Age range

Eight to eleven.

Group size

Any.

What you need

Examples of indexes, plenty of ticket-size pieces of paper, a few pages of text (this could be children's work or a small printed book without an index), a word processor (optional), pencils.

What to do

Introduce the activity by showing the children a few examples of different indexes – including an encyclopaedia index if you have one. Explain that indexing is a very skilled and complex task and that there are people who work as professional indexers. Explain to the children some basic indexing procedures.

- Take a brief look at the whole text and read one or two pages to find out what the text is about and get an idea of the range of principal content nouns.
- Decide on an average number of content nouns to be selected from each page.
- Proceed through the text page by page and for each page select and copy out the principal content words (invariably nouns), putting one word on each ticket with the relevant page number.

- When the whole text has been scanned and a full collection of content word tickets has been made, set them out in alphabetical order. Put them first into initial letter groups and then order them within each group. When there are several tickets for one word these can be put in numerical order.
- Write or type out the arranged list, making sure that repeated words are only entered once but listing all the page numbers in numerical order.
- Finally, attach the list to the end of the text.

Having explained the basic process the children can have a go at compiling an index for a book that they have made or for some other short information book where an index is lacking.

Name books

Objective
To promote a knowledge of names and noun varieties.

Age range
Seven to nine.

Group size
Any.

What you need
Small notebooks, dictionaries, pencils, felt-tipped pens or crayons.

What to do
This is an on-going short activity which could be carried out over many days, or several weeks. It could be used as a regular start-the-day activity or as a brief fill-in session. Each day announce a different category of nouns and ask the children to write down examples which fit this grouping. The group categories should be as varied as possible; for example, boys' names, surnames, names of a particular group of animals or plants, planets, days and months, desk contents, noises, favourite foods, football teams, games, nouns with particular initial letters or containing particular letter patterns, homophones, synonyms and so on. Suggest that they limit the lists to about twelve words and that they add small illustrations on the facing page.

Planets	Plants
Mercury	grass
Venus	nettles
Earth	dandelions
Mars	daisies
Jupiter	cabbages
Saturn	roses
Uranus	yucca
Neptune	sunflower
Pluto	rhubarb

Follow-up
Invite the children to finish off the booklets, by adding a list of contents and a new cover.

Referring (pronouns)

Pronouns are substitutes for nouns. They usually fall into place quite naturally and don't need much introduction except, perhaps, when they are joined to verb contractions. The first person pronoun 'I' takes pride of place as the only one always to be composed of a capital letter wherever it finds itself in any sentence. Third person pronouns (he, she, it, they, him, her and them) become particularly useful for taking the place of nouns which would otherwise be rather clumsily repeated.

The great I am

Objective
To practise using and writing the first person singular pronoun 'I'.

Age range
Five to seven.

Group size
Any.

What you need
Paper, pencils, some prepared activity word cards with inscriptions like 'ride a bike', 'do up shoe laces', 'peel an orange', and 'hang upside down'.

What to do
This activity offers a straightforward opportunity for some personal boasting and self-assertion. It can start with a discussion about what special physical actions or feats different children can do, leading from questions like:

- Who can ride a bike?
- Who can do up shoe laces?
- Who can peel an orange?
- Who can hang upside down, run backwards or read upside down?

Praise the children for their claims and point out that everybody has their own special different skills and achievements. Depending upon their age and ability, ask the children to write one or several statements about their particular capabilities, starting with a line such as 'I am great' or 'I am the great John Brown'. If necessary, give the children the word cards to help them compose their statements. Display the pieces of writing together in a book or on the wall and give them a general title such as 'Our great class'.

Guess who's who!

Objective
To make simple profiles of people and use appropriate personal pronouns.

Age range
Six to ten.

Group size
Any.

What you need
Pictures and photographs of people, an example of a written profile (see below), paper, pencils, felt-tipped pens, crayons or paints.

What to do
Describe a person using a pronoun rather than a name and then ask the children to guess who he or she might be. The person could be somebody the children know well or it might be somebody chosen from a collection of portrait pictures. After you have done this two or three times, ask the children to describe somebody they know in the same way. You could then show the children a card on which you have written an anonymous profile with a flap at the bottom revealing the person's name.

Suggest to the children that they paint or draw a picture of somebody, but not to reveal who that person is. They should also write an anonymous description to place under the portrait. Finally, ask them to write out the person's name and hide it under a flap at the bottom.

Display all the work, making a portrait gallery.

Demonstrating this and that

Objective
To show and practise the use of demonstrative pronouns.

Age range
Six to nine.

Group size
Individuals or pairs.

What you need
Special collections of objects or photos.

What to do
Tell the children that they are going to have a chance to show and describe special collections of items. Demonstrate the procedure first by holding up a series of objects, announcing what they are, and then saying at least one thing about them. For example: 'This is an old penny. It has a picture of Queen Victoria' or 'This is an old pound note. It belonged to my mother'.

Ask the children to prepare short demonstrations of their own. Give them some time to think about what collections they are going to make or bring in. Explain that they will be required to announce each item as well as have something to say about it. After each demonstration, invite the audience to ask questions.

Follow-up
Ask the children to label their collections and display them around the classroom.

What is it?

Objective
To make riddles by playing on the use of the pronoun 'it'.

Age range
Seven to eleven.

Group size
Any.

What you need
Pencils, cards (about postcard size).

What to do
Start by posing a few different riddles. There are a number of different types you could use, for example:
• Where 'it' refers to a concrete object, for instance, 'It has a strong smell. It is round. It can be peeled. It grows in the ground. It goes with sausages. It begins with o' (onion).
• Ones which refer to abstract ideas like time, energy, anger, mood, hope, friendship and so on.
• Ones which refer to particular persons or animals (as we sometimes do when referring to someone not in favour).

Ask the children to make up some riddles of their own. Write a selection of possible subjects on some cards and then ask the children, in turn, to pick one and use it to make their riddles. Suggest that they write their riddles on the reverse side of each card. Draw the children's attention to how 'it is' can be contracted to 'it's' and that the apostrophe is used to show the place of the missing letter.

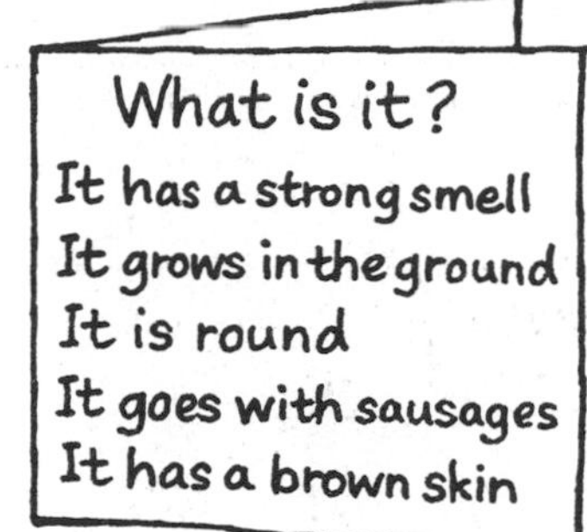

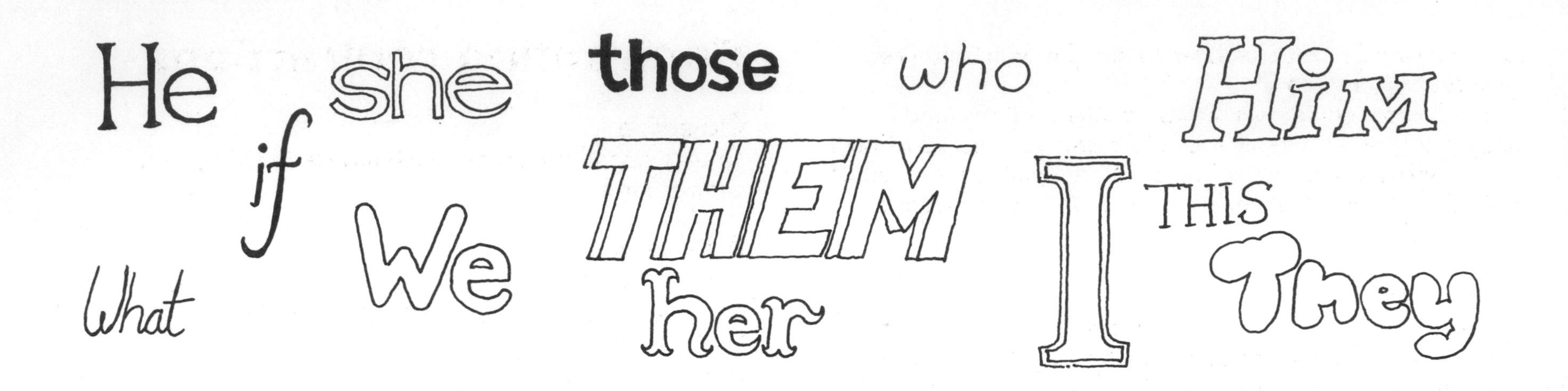

Naming no names

Objective
To tell or write stories using pronouns and anonymous terms instead of names.

Age range
Seven to ten.

Group size
Any.

What you need
Paper, pencils (optional).

What to do
Ask the children to tell or write down stories about an anonymous character. As the character is anonymous they must use pronouns instead of a name. Explain that the rest of the group has to guess or work out who the character is.

Us and them

Objective
To develop the use of principal pronouns.

Age range
Seven to eleven.

Group size
Any.

What you need
A good selection of the principal pronouns written on the board or on a chart (I, you, he, she, it, we, they, who, what, this, that, these, those, me, him, her, us, them, mine, yours, his, hers, its, ours, theirs), paper, pencils.

What to do
Start by showing the children the collection of words and challenging them to say what is special about them. Are they naming words? Explain that they are known as

pronouns and ask the children to sort the words into two groups, 'us' or 'them'.

The sorting out is bound to be a little arbitrary and subject to the feelings of each child and you should respect this. In making their choices the children will have to reflect a little on the functions of each word and the concept of 'them and us'.

Follow-up

Older children could develop the idea of 'us' and 'them' groups, with discussions about all the social implications. Ask them to divide a piece of paper into two columns – 'us' and 'them'. Suggest that on the 'us' side the children list all the different kinds of groupings to which they belong and opposite each one an equivalent group outside it. The 'us' groupings might include playground gangs, classroom groups, classes, teams, close family, wider family, clubs, streets, neighbourhoods, districts, countries, continents, species and so on.

Confronting contractions

Objective

To understand pronouns which induce auxiliary verb contractions.

Age range

Eight to eleven.

Group size

Any.

What you need

Paper,pencils.

What to do

This activity will help the children to tackle the question of learning how to write the contractions which commonly follow many of the pronouns like 'I'm', 'you're', 'she'll', 'it's', 'we'll', 'they're' and so on. These forms of contractions are particularly common in speech but are also reproduced in writing. Point out to the children the form of each particular contraction and let them practise making sequences of similarly patterned sentences. Ask them to make as many sentences as they can which follow on from particular openings and, if possible, which are associated with a particular circumstance. They might like to invent songs, for example:

- It's a long way to Brighton.

It's a long way to...

- I'd better do my work.

I'd better eat my greens.
I'd better...

- What's the matter with you?

What's the matter with me?...

Describing (adjectives)

Adjectives are usually defined as 'describing words'. We can also refer to them as epithets, words which express qualities or attributes of nouns. Adjectives add precision and refinement to the skill of naming and make for vivid, stylish language.

Varieties

Objective
To select adjectives imaginatively.

Age range
Five to nine.

Group size
Any.

What you need
Pencils, paper, felt-tipped pens, crayons, dictionaries.

What to do
With younger children, ask them to think about as many different varieties of a particular item as they can and to collect words which distinguish them. For example, you could ask them to think of different adjectives to describe a single subject such as cars, cats, monsters, houses, people, and so on. Encourage the children to think about the shape, size, colour, texture, weight and character traits of their subjects, for example: big dogs, spotty dogs, red dogs, fat dogs and so on. Put a range of collectively suggested adjectives on the board and then ask the children, individually or in pairs, to make, write up and illustrate their own variety lists.

Give older children the more challenging task of making up adjective alphabets to describe particular subjects. Ask them to find at least two adjectives for each letter, for example agile angry cats, beautiful blue cats, creepy cringing cats, dangerous daft cats....

Encourage the children to write out their alphabets, illustrate them and make them into booklets.

Follow-up

Invite the children to create alliterative alphabets, such as the following: amazing appetising apples; big boisterous boys; clever cheerful chimps and so on.

Develop the idea further by asking the children to use other parts of speech: an awesome American alligator ate apples assiduously;

big bad boys break bottles boisterously.

A sea of faces

Objective

To find a multitude of different adjectives to describe facial appearances.

Age range

Five to eight.

Group size

Any.

What you need

Pencils, large sheets of paper, scissors, felt-tipped pens, crayons, sticky labels.

What to do

Discuss with the children the idea that every person's face is different. Follow this by drawing a cartoon face on the board and asking the children to say what kind of face it is. Write the adjectives they give underneath the picture. Then ask one of the children to draw a different face and ask the other children to describe it. After a few more examples tell the children that they are now going to make their own large 'sea' of different faces. Each child can draw a face on paper and attach an adjective label to it. All the face pictures and labels can then be mounted as one large display.

Adjective riddles

Objective
To make simple riddles out of sets of adjectives which describe particular objects or beings.

Age range
Five to eight.

Group size
Pairs or small groups.

What you need
A selection of everyday objects such as fruit, toys, clothes, utensils and so on; a screen or a cover, postcard-size cards, pencils.

What to do
Hold an object behind your back and after you have given the children a list of appropriate adjectives, ask them to guess what it is. Let the children try describing their own objects, prompting a wide selection of adjectives – to describe size, shape, colour, texture, weight, feel, value, utility, attractiveness and so on.

Develop this idea by making riddle cards with descriptive adjectives on one side and names or identifying pictures on the reverse side. To make this more fun and challenging, encourage deceptive descriptions as in the classic children's joke, 'What has a trunk and is happy and grey?' Answer: 'A mouse going on holiday'.

What is happy and grey and has a trunk?

In one word

Objective
To appreciate and become selective of 'choice' single adjectives.

Age range
Five to eleven.

Group size
Any.

What you need
Paper, pencils.

What to do
Discuss with the children the idea of using descriptive words to sum up the essential character of people. As examples, remind them of the seven dwarves (Grumpy, Happy, Sleepy, Sneezy, Dopey, Bashful and Doc) and the Mister Men. You could also give the children a few newly invented examples (perhaps of other members of staff) to guess. Then give the children a list of people (members of the class, members of staff, television personalities, for

example) or things (foods, animals, school subjects and activities, books, television programmes, sports, favourite things, times, places, and so on). Ask the children to select a *different* apt adjective to go with each person or item. Be prepared to change the adjectives around many times.

Wanted

Objective
To use adjectives to create precise descriptions.

Age range
Six to ten.

Group size
Any.

What you need
Large sheets of paper, pencils, felt-tipped pens.

What to do
Discuss with the children why they think precise descriptions are needed – for example, for finding, say, a dangerous criminal or missing person. What particular features do they think need to be described? Write their suggestions on the board. For example: colour of eyes, height, colour and nature of hair, facial expression, shape of the head, stoutness, age, colours and styles of clothes, character and so on.

Talk with the children about posters which describe missing or wanted people and ask them to invent some of their own. Alternatively they could describe a missing pet. Encourage the children to use adjectives precisely.

Embroidering

Objective
To promote the idea that adjectives (and adverbs) can sometimes be considered as extra words to convey more description and feeling.

Age range
Seven to eleven.

Group size
Any.

What you need
Photocopiable page 118 or other samples of printed text (reproduced and enlarged, if possible), a word processor if available, paper, pencils.

What to do
Together with the children look at a sample of text and ask them whether they can suggest any single new words which they could add to make it a little more descriptive. After a few suggestions have been given, discuss what kind of words these are (there might be few adverbs as well as adjectives). Show them the traditional editing procedures for indicating such insertions. When all the children understand the general idea of making such additions, ask them how many they can do themselves and see how far they can change the original text in this way.

Children with access to a word processor can obviously carry out this task more neatly and instantaneously. Those editing text by hand may well find that they need to make a new copy of the text. The exercise is probably more fun if you encourage the children to be imaginative in their choice of adjectives and even to mock gently the original text.

Follow-up
- Let the children do this activity using hyperbole with superlative adjectives (many of the books of Roald Dahl, for instance, provide vivid examples for this kind of style).
- Discuss and let the children try out the possibilities of adding similes instead of adjectives.
- Encourage the children to try out the possibilities of adding relative clauses.

Good alternatives

Objectives
To confront the issue of over-used adjectives and to find descriptive alternatives.

Age range
Seven to eleven.

Group size
Any.

What you need
Large sheets of paper, pencils, felt-tipped pens, thesauri, dictionaries.

What to do
Discuss with the children the current favourite adjectives for indicating approval and disapproval. Write one of the more popular examples on the board, circle it and add radiating lines. You can then discuss what alternative adjectives convey the same sentiment and write them on the board to make a web. Ask the children to look in dictionaries and thesauri for any more alternatives to add. When a complete or near-complete chart has been agreed upon, ask a small group of children to make a poster version for classroom reference and display.

Follow-up
• Apply the same approach to distinguish different nuances of other over-familiar words, for example, great – famous, important, distinguished, enormous, heavy, admirable, high standard and highly enjoyable.

• Let the children make fun of a particularly over-used adjective by doing a piece of writing and using it to excess. They could even make fun of any adjective by deliberately repeating it (as in Charles Causley's poem 'The Jolly Hunter', in several anthologies including *Strictly Private* by Roger McGough, Puffin Books).

Aspirations

Objective

To dwell on the appeal of future expectations and how they might be described.

Age range

Seven to ten.

Group size

Any.

What you need

Paper, pencils.

What to do

Discuss with the children what they want to be like when they are older or grown up. Ask them to try and come up with one word suggestions and to write down some of their thoughts and aspirations, following a formula something like this:

When I grow up I will be rich and famous.
My house will be ...
My car will be ...
My children will be ...
My life will be ...
The world will be ...

Explain that they should provide one or two adjectives for each aspiration.

Follow-up

- Let the children make up multiple-choice questionnaires based on the above format.
- Extend the idea by suggesting that the children use similes. For example: 'When I'm old I'll be as wise as ... as strong as ...'.

Specifying (articles)

Articles fulfil a rather similar role to adjectives and are sometimes regarded as weak forms of adjectives. They have a subtle and precise function of indicating whether things are being described in specific or general terms. They really speak for themselves, 'speak' being the operative word, as their correct use naturally develops from talking and listening attentively and exactingly. In speech, too, 'the' and 'a' can be given variable pronunciations and emphases. The chapter contains just one semi-analytical activity which draws attention to the existence and principal functioning of articles.

Definitely or indefinitely?

Objective
To create an awareness of definite and indefinite articles and their specifying roles.

Age range
Nine to eleven.

Group size
Any.

What you need
Paper, pencils.

What to do
Write the three articles 'the', 'a' and 'an' as a group of words on the board. 'Some' is used as an article but can have a stronger adjectival sense denoting degrees of quantity, and it can also be used as a pronoun. For the purpose of simpler analysis it is not being included initially in the group. Ask the children to suggest any explanations for what they might think is special about these three words, prompting them, if necessary, with questions like:

- What kind of other words do they go with?
- What do articles do to these words?
- Are they more like adjectives than nouns?
- Can they appear at the beginning of sentences?
- Can they appear at the end of sentences?
- What's the difference between saying 'I want an apple' and 'I want the apple'?
- Why don't we say 'I want *a* apple'?
- Are there any words that do the same thing as these words?
- What about the words 'some' and 'any'?

Introduce and explain the terms definite article and indefinite article. Then ask the children to demonstrate some statements which will illustrate the different functions of the two types of article. These might be produced along the following lines:

- Here is *an* apple. It's *the* apple I have chosen for you.
- Here is *a* banana. It's *the* best of *the* bunch.
- Here are *some* cherries. These are *the* cherries which I picked.
- Here is *a* drink. It's *the* drink of all drinks.

Reacting (verbs)

A meaningful utterance nearly always has a verb as a key component. Verbs *enable* sequences of words to stand on their own and make complete sense (and full sentences). They are often described as 'doing words' but this is rather inadequate: 'doing or being words' is a little more helpful. The following activities highlight the range of verbs and the variety of forms in which they can be employed.

Cat and mouse

Objective
To compose a series of short repeating sentences where the verb is continually being substituted.

Age range
Six to nine.

Group size
Any.

What you need
Paper, pencils, scissors, card.

What to do
On the board write 'The cat... the mouse'. Then ask the children for ideas about what can happen between the cat and the mouse, in other words, what different verbs can be placed in the middle to make a sentence. Let the children start by using verbs in the present tense, such as 'smells', 'goes near', 'touches', 'tickles', 'plays with', 'chases', 'runs after' and 'tricks'.

The children could write the list of possible substitutions as one long sequence of 'It... It...', inserting a word each time.

When the children have got used to the present tense, ask them to do something similar using the past and future tenses.

Follow-up
- Let the children repeat the above exercise in reverse to show what the mouse might do to the cat.
- Encourage the children to develop an action-packed story by having the cat and mouse alternatively as subject and object.
- Suggest that the children make up comic strips with the above.

Using initiative

Objective
To promote initiative ideas in a variety of situations and thereby make use of a wide range of verbs.

Age range
Eight to eleven.

Group size
Any.

What you need
Paper, pencils.

What to do
Let the children consider a challenge such as one of the following:
- Ten/101 things to do with an orange/a cat/a pencil/a brother/a piece of paper/a book/a bully.
- How to be a good friend/a nuisance/a creep.
- How to win at marbles/football/sports.
- Ten ways to escape boredom.
- How to look after a pet.

Ask the children to discuss and suggest a range of initiatives to meet the particular challenge, using as many verbs as possible. This could take the form of an oral quiz game or you could ask the children to compile lists.

Follow-up
Invite the children to make lists of 'dos and don'ts' favourite hobbies, activities and so on. With the children's help, edit the lists and make them into booklets or leaflets.

Action stations

Objectives
To promote familiarity with the written form of verbs and the idea that actions are associated with verbs.

Age range
Five to six.

Group size
Eight children.

What you need
Action cards (see photocopiable page 119), card, scissors, adhesive, space to act.

What to do
Stick the copy from photocopiable page 119 on some card and cut it up into separate cards. Introduce the cards one by one to the children and then shuffle them and place them face downwards on a table. Ask a volunteer to pick one out without showing it to anyone else and then to mime the action. The rest of the group should try to guess what action is on the card.

Follow-up
- Give the cards to a pair of children to arrange in sequence and make up their own action story.
- Let the children create their own pictures for each action and combine them to make a book or wall display.

Behaviour

Objectives

To link commonly-known nouns with their usually associated verbs and to dwell on the idea of characteristic behaviour.

Age range

Six to nine.

Group size

Any.

What you need

Paper, pencils.

What to do

Call out, one by one, a series of common nouns in their plural form, including different kinds of people, animals and objects. For each one, ask a child to suggest what this person or animal generally does or what happens to them. If possible, try to create sequences of associations which have a natural progression and a conclusion, maybe returning to the first person. For example:

- Mice squeak.
- Cats purr.
- Dogs bark.
- Babies cry.
- Mothers work.
- Teachers teach.
- Books open.
- Pencils are ready.
- And we write.

Encourage the children to compile compositions like this and write them out. Alternatively, you could put a range of plural nouns on the board and ask the children to make their own lists of associated actions or behaviour.

Follow-up

- Let the children have fun by making up a fantasy list of associations where inanimate objects 'come alive'.
- Use a past tense – What did they do? – Or indicate potential – What can they do?

All go!

Objective
To make commentaries which convey action-packed events and thereby use a variety of verbs.

Age range
Seven to eleven.

Group size
Any.

What you need
Paper, pencils.

What to do
Consider and discuss with the children occasions when events become especially hectic and when we seem to be continually on the go – 'getting ready for school', ' a school morning', 'a busy weekend', 'an excursion' or 'Christmas Eve'. Then ask them to think of and relate the series of actions or happenings that might take place on a chosen occasion. Give an example such as, 'A dash to the shops':
- Grab the purse.
- Pick up a bag.
- Put on coat.
- Rush out of door.
- Dive into car . . . and so on.

Invite the children to make up 'all go' accounts along similar lines. Explain that they could be produced in list form as above, as a kind of poem, or they could be written down as one long piece of punctuated prose: I grab my purse, pick up a bag, put on my coat....

Follow-up
- Ask the children to do the exercise in the past or future tense.
- Let the children make it into a comic strip.

Qualifying (adverbs)

'Adding to verbs' (and to adjectives) is precisely what adverbs are about. Their special role is to modify or qualify the sense conveyed by verbs or adjectives. Their careful use affects the finer tuning of language skill. Adjectives can quite often be used as adverbs or adjusted in form (by adding 'ly', for instance) for such use. Sometimes, too, prepositions appear to take adverbial roles (as in 'sit down' or 'come in', for instance). Adverbs, therefore, are not always easy to identify and the development of language skill is not necessarily well served by too much attention to unravelling particular roles.

The following activities focus on the range of linguistic adjustment that adverbs can bring.

How it's done

Objective
To demonstrate physically how particular actions (verbs) can be modified by applying a variety of adverbs.

Age range
Six to eight.

Group size
Any.

What you need
A large open space.

What to do
This activity is probably best done in a PE lesson. Start by asking the children to follow your directions and tell them to do the following: 'Sit up! Sit down! Sit comfortably! Sit uncomfortably! Sit still! Sit restlessly! Sit quietly! Sit noisily! Sit back!'

After a few examples, ask the children to suggest and demonstrate a few more different ones of their own. Then try the procedure with some other verbs like 'walk', 'run', 'stand', 'look', 'talk' and 'sing'.

Follow-up
Invite the children to make up charts or booklets to show different ways of 'How it's done' for a variety of activities. Suggest that they illustrate them with stick people or cartoon drawings.

Maybe sometimes always never

Objective
To compose a short series of sentences which focus on individual adverbs.

Age range
Six to nine.

Group size
Any.

What you need
Paper, pencils.

What to do
Start by collectively composing a series of sentences which all begin with one adverb, such as, sometimes. Provide the first two lines and then ask for suggestions of other possible lines to follow. For example:

- Sometimes we are happy.
- Sometimes we are sad.
- Sometimes we are naughty.
- Sometimes we go mad.
- Sometimes...

When they fully understand the idea, ask the children to make up their own versions using the same adverb or another such as 'perhaps', 'of course', 'usually', 'occasionally', 'always', 'never', 'hardly ever' and so on. Point out to them that the adverb could be in the middle or at the end of the sentence as well as at the beginning.

Shades of grey

Objective
To demonstrate how gradual modifications of adjectives can be produced, often with the help of adverbs.

Age range
Seven to ten.

Group size
Any.

What you need
Long strips of paper (about 5cm x 1m), scrap paper, pencils.

What to do
At one end of the board write 'black' and at the other end write 'white'. Ask the children to name any colour that comes in between these two words. When 'grey' is suggested, ask the children to tell you different shades such as light, very light, silvery, middling, dark, extremely dark, charcoal and so on. Write the names of the different suggested shades on the board, placing them in relative positions between 'black' and 'white'.

Discuss with the children the fact that many adjectives can have different shades of meaning. When the children have understood the general idea of moderating adjectives (both by adding adverbs and by changing the adjective itself), ask them to make their own 'shades of meaning' strips. Explain that they could either try this with other colours (the variety of greens is good to do in early summer) or the degrees of difference between antonym adjectives such as beautiful and ugly, exciting and boring, hot and cold, difficult and easy.

Follow-up
Instead of using adverbs, ask the children to try using a scale of similes, for instance, as greedy as a mouse/pig/horse/hungry lion.

Absolutely amazing reviews

Objective
To develop a good use of adverbially-prefaced adjectives.

Age range
Seven to eleven.

Group size
Any.

What you need
Photocopiable page 120 (either in full or partially blanked out), pencils.

What to do
There are two parts to this activity. First, ask the children to build up a repertoire of reviewing adjectives (single words describing a film, book, television programme, sports match, and so on) together with a collection of adverbs which might qualify them. You could do this together as a class or give each child a copy of page 120 and ask them to complete it.

Your aim should be to make the children aware of the hackneyed phrases which such reviews often use and to extend their descriptive/critical capacities.

Second, let the children have the opportunity to make pithy two or three word reactions to particular events and occasions in the form of:

- a general television review where the children are asked to make a list of current television programmes (perhaps distinguishing different channels or particular viewing times) and give each one a *different* reviewing comment;
- diary entries where the children keep personal journals or diaries with pithy comments written alongside a short timetable of events to make a refreshing change from more extended prose;
- a review of a special event where the children write full critical reviews of such an occasion, headlined by a pithy two or three word reaction. (Deciding on an emotive headline first can help with the content of the review.) With the children's help, place the reviews together with some of the choice descriptions or criticisms highlighted or use them as slogans as on a theatre poster;
- 'send ups' where, the children use to excess certain adverbs in order to make fun of what is being considered and of such excessive language itself;
- a full school report where the children are asked to list every aspect of school (subjects, parts of building, dinners, playtimes, and so on) and then apply a different two word comment to each one.

Possibly Probably doubtfully

Especially, really, actually

Objectives

To consider some of the more commonly used adverbs in everyday speech and writing and to experiment with their use.

Age range

Nine to eleven.

Group size

Any.

What you need

Copies of a page of printed prose (preferably slightly enlarged to average handwriting size), paper, pencils.

What to do

Ask the children to suggest and elicit some well-used adverbs, especially ones used to introduce sentences: firstly, however, next, then, when, afterwards, finally, especially, particularly, brilliantly, actually, quite, not and well. When you have collected a dozen or so, either ask the children to write short stories using as many of these words as often as possible, or give them a piece of copied prose and ask them to insert as many of these words as possible into the text, making it a little ridiculous. Ask the children to consider different positions within sentences where the adverbs might be placed and to decide which reads the best and makes the most sense.

If the issue of split infinitives arises, be flexible about it, though you could point out that this is a case where speech and written language can be different.

Let the children swap their texts and invite their comments.

Follow-up

- Let the children cut out superfluous adverbs from particular pieces of text or from the examples they have created.
- Encourage the children to experiment with some poetic word play by writing the same sentence several times but with a particular adverb in a different place each time. Give them the following example to consider:

Amazingly the owl and the pussy cat went to sea in a beautiful pea green boat.

The owl and, amazingly, the pussy cat went to sea in a beautiful pea green boat.

The owl and the amazingly pussy cat went to sea in a beautiful pea green boat.

The owl and the pussy cat amazingly went to sea in a beautiful pea green boat.

The owl and the pussy cat went amazingly to sea in a beautiful pea green boat.

The owl and the pussy cat went to sea amazingly in a beautiful pea green boat.

The owl and the pussy cat went to sea in an amazingly beautiful pea green boat.

The owl and the pussy cat went to sea in a beautiful, amazingly pea green boat.

The owl and the pussy cat went to sea in a beautiful pea green boat amazingly.

Directing (prepositions)

We use prepositions to give direction and shape to what we say and write. They give an idea of the relationships of time, space or belonging. The following activities highlight their variety and demonstrate their functions.

Positioning words

Objectives
To become familiar with positional prepositions and to place them aptly.

Age range
Five to seven.

Group size
Up to eight children.

What you need
Photocopiable page 121, an empty box, pencils, paper.

What to do
Using photocopiable page 121 make the stand-up word labels. Place a box or container on a table in front of the children and show them each word label one by one. Ask the children individually to place the labels in relation to the box on the table, Therefore, the label with 'in' on it should be inside the box, the 'under' one could be unfolded and put under the box and so on. Once the children understand the idea, ask them to work in pairs and make their own preposition arrangements, maybe in other parts of the classroom.

Following on from this, try a two-dimensional pictorial approach by drawing a shape in the middle of a piece of paper and, with the children's help, writing the names of prepositions in and around it in appropriate positions. At this stage, ask the children if they can come up with any other positional prepositions, for example, 'near' 'away from', 'far from', 'alongside' and 'close to'.

Follow-up
Encourage the children to play a version of 'hunt the thimble' where they have to hide a small object or sweet and find out where it is by asking questions involving prepositions.

Missing!

Objective
To produce some imaginative ideas about where missing things might be found.

Age range
Seven to ten.

Group size
Any.

What you need
Pencils, paper.

What to do
A good way to introduce this activity is to make out that you have lost something and start asking yourself questions such as the following:

- 'Help! My pen is missing!'
- 'Is it in my pocket?'
- 'Is it on my desk?'
- 'Is it in my desk?'
- 'Has it fallen behind the radiator?'
- 'Is under my desk?'
- 'Has it taken a walk outside?'
- 'Has it wandered into the staff room?'
- 'Has it wandered into somebody else's pocket?'
- 'Has it gone to the moon?'
- 'Oh, where has my pencil gone?'

Discuss with the children different things that they have lost, including such concepts as sense, brains, my imagination, all my energy, friends, pets and so on.

Then encourage them to create a piece of imaginative writing on the above lines.

Getting lost

Objective
To exploit the idea of giving directions and using prepositions in an imaginative way.

Age range
Seven to eleven.

Group size
Any.

What you need
Pencils, paper.

What to do
Discuss with the children what it is like to lose your way and ask them to describe an occasion when this has happened to them.

Suggest that they do a piece of writing about 'How to get absolutely lost' by making up a series of crazy confusing directions. Prompt them by eliciting and writing on the board a variety of directional prepositions, such as 'through', 'up', 'over', 'along', 'between', 'under', 'beneath', 'left by ...', 'right at ...', 'beyond', 'behind', 'past', 'in', 'on' and 'to'. Ask them to finish with a punch line about what happens to them in the end – whether they remain lost or not.

Follow-up
- Let the children produce an accurate series of directions to end up in mystery places known only to the writer. They should then ask readers to try them out or work out where they lead to.
- Ask the children to make diagrammatic mazes or real or model obstacle courses which require directional instructions for moving through.

Which way?

Objective
To make travelling stories which use a wide variety of prepositions.

Age range
Six to nine.

Group size
Any.

What you need
Examples of good stories, such as *Bears in the Night* by S. and J. Berenstain (Picture Lions) or *On my Way to School* Celia Berridge (Andre Deutsch), which have accumulative adventures involving sequences of prepositional directions; paper, pencils.

What to do
Read one or two stories to the children and encourage them to act them out.

Suggest other characters which could make short adventurous journeys for instance, a classroom pet, a fictional scallywag, any creature or possibly an inanimate object. When a few ideas have been discussed, ask the children to try and write their own stories on these lines. Put a selection of directional prepositions on the board as an aid.

Follow-up
- Let the children edit and illustrate the stories to produce books or zigzag pull-out charts. Older children might even be able to make flaps and pop-up devices.
- Invite the children to dramatise and present their stories to an audience.

Extending (conjunctions)

Conjunctions are parts of speech used to link words, phrases, clauses or sentences together. We use them when we want to extend what we are saying. The word 'and' is the most widely used and the most straightforward of all the conjunctions although, together with 'or', it is one of very few words rarely to be found at the beginning of sentences. Other words used as conjunctions include 'but', 'if', 'when', 'before', 'either... or', 'since', 'because', 'until', 'although', 'unless', 'while', and 'after'. These words can also take on adverbial or prepositional roles.

Again and again and again...

Objective
To use repeatedly particular words and thereby practise writing fluently, using 'and' abundantly.

Age range
Five to eight.

Group size
Any.

What you need
Pencils, paper.

What to do
There are various ways of carrying out this activity.

- Repeated action stories where the children make up simple stories in which they repeat a verb many times and finally reach a conclusion. For instance: 'He walked and walked and walked and walked and walked and walked and walked and walked... until his feet dropped off'.
- Circular everlasting word chains where the children write out words which lend themselves to being repeated endlessly; for example: 'forever and forever and forever and forever...' or 'on and on, and on and on and on...'.
- Describing abundances where the children write short sentences about what they notice or desire in abundance. For example: 'I would like lots and lots and lots and lots... of chips'. or 'I looked up at the sky and saw stars and stars and stars and stars and stars...'.

Food combinations

Objectives
To compile combinations of items that we enjoy having together and to practise using the conjunctions 'and' and 'or'.

Age range
Five to seven.

Group size
Any.

What you need
Paper, pencils, felt-tipped pens.

What to do
Start a discussion about things that are commonly associated as combinations such as 'boys and girls', 'fish and chips', 'salt and pepper', and particular classroom friendships. Ask the children to write down original combinations of food and illustrate them to make a special classroom menu. You could even follow this up with a feast in the classroom. Draw the children's attention to the different ways of arranging two-or more part combinations with the use of commas and only one conjunction, for example: 'chicken and tomato sauce' or 'nuts, currants, raisins and cheese'.

One sentence stories

Objective
To make short anecdotal stories which require the extending of a single sentence.

Age range
Five to eight.

Group size
Any.

What you need
Paper, pencils.

What to do
Tell the children that together they are going to make up some very short stories. Start by giving them an opening clause followed by a conjunction and asking for suggestions for how the sentence/story might finish. For instance:
- I went to the zoo and....
- I went to the zoo but....
- I went to the zoo because....
- I went to the zoo although....
- I was on my way to the zoo when.....

Follow-up
Show the children how short sequences of events or descriptions can be told in a single sentence using commas and a final conjunction: 'I went down the road, over a bridge, past the shops and arrived at the cinema'.

Invite the children to try and make some three- or four-part sentence stories of their own.

Constructing sentences

Sentence construction is our basic method of using and arranging words to create meaning. We do this by discovering and using grammatical procedures without necessarily being aware of them and their complexity. We are seemingly born with a natural capacity to use grammar and generate sentences of our own right from the start. It is a highly creative operation. The range of possible sentences is infinite and this requires us all to be continually inventive in how we construct them.

A sentence expresses a complete thought, be it statement, a command or a question. It has a distinct rounded entity which can or should be easily recognised. In speech this is signalled by intonation and a slight final pause. In writing it is marked out by a starting capital letter and a final punctuating stop. Mastery of sound sentence construction develops from clear thinking and from the natural urge to sort things out in one's mind into small comprehensible units of thought or series of such units – though, of course, our thoughts can and will easily run away with us in a disordered way. The quest for order and easy comprehension underlies the activities in this third chapter.

Ideas for a practical sentence making workshop are outlined and there follows a series of activities based on a variety of linguistic purposes such as exclaiming, commanding, stating, questioning and explaining. These introduce contexts which oblige the use and development of a considerable range of grammatical structures. Finally, we finish with a few ideas relating more directly to punctuation and capitalisation and introduce some more specific editing techniques.

The sentence workshop

Objective
To play, experiment and work with constructing simple sentences out of ready-made word cards.

Age range
Five to nine.

Group size
Up to six children.

What you need
A long table, white paper, coloured sugar paper, pencils, felt-tipped pens, six boxes (shoe box size) differently, coloured and labelled for the different parts of speech: nouns (the largest box, preferably subdivided with sections for proper nouns, single common nouns, plural nouns, and pronouns), verbs (ideally subdivided into two sections for verbs in their simple present and simple past forms) adjectives and articles (possibly one each for these) adverbs, prepositions and interjections; different coloured word cards/tickets to match the boxes, photocopiable page 122, card. (NB: the Breakthrough to Literacy 'Sentence Maker' equipment can easily be adapted for much of this work.)

What to do
Set up the workshop. Use photocopiable page 122 to help you write out an initial working collection of word cards and make a number of sentence racks from folded card.

The sentence workshop can be used to carry out many operations. But the examples given below can be used to demonstrate how sentences can gradually be built up.

- Double acts

Ask the children to see how many two word phrases they can say taken from just two different boxes. Let them try putting present tense verbs before various adverbs, and also plural nouns or pronouns in front of verbs. For example: come quickly, come slowly, come anyhow, come here.

Ask the children to display their compositions on sentence racks or to stick them on to larger sheets of paper.

- Three partners

Let the children see how many things they can say combining three different parts of sentences using particular colour sequences, for example: pronouns/plural nouns + verbs + adverbs or adjectives + plural nouns + verbs.

Invite them to find out how many three-part different colour sequences are possible.

• A substitution game
Show the children how to make and arrange a sentence of about four or five words on the sentence rack. Explain to them that each player has to change at least one of the words by replacing it with another of the same colour. If necessary, they can add new words to the collections as they are needed. As part of each turn, the children can make one colour change and also one addition or subtraction. Invite the children to record the successive sentences to create a patterned poem like the following:

I like bananas and cheese.
Monkeys like bananas and *trees.*
Elephants like bananas *on* trees.
Elephants *eat* bananas on trees.
They eat bananas *at school.*
We sing songs at school.

• Follow the pattern
Give the children a particular colour/word part sequence, for example: article, noun, verb, preposition, article, noun. Ask them to see how many things they can say following exactly that pattern. See if they can make up a number of such sentences into a playful and meaningful word jingle.

Article	**Noun**	**Verb**	**Preposition**	**Article**	**Noun**
The	cow	jumped	over	the	moon
The	cat	sat	on	the	mat
An	elephant	walked	beside	a	mouse
The	house	stood	on	the	hill

• Storying
For any real 'free-er' story composition, the finding and placing of appropriate cards can be quite cumbersome. To alleviate this, a quantity of blank cards which are ready to be ascribed are useful and it is probably best just to keep to a limited number of categorised words (say nouns, verbs, adjectives and 'all others'). This is an interesting exercise to try once to demonstrate how complex grammatical patterning rapidly becomes, even with the simplest of narrative forms.

Exclamations

Sounding off

Objectives
To practise and exploit the idea of using interjections and making single word sentences.

Age range
Seven to eleven.

Group size
Any.

What you need
Paper, pencils, felt-tipped pens, comics which have an abundance of interjections or other single words used in an expletive way.

What to do
Start by addressing the class or group using a number of single word expletives – 'Oh! Look! Here! James! Ouch! Quiet! No!'

Ask the children to comment on this mode of talking and to suggest any other single words which make complete sense when said on their own. Discuss with them where written single words can be seen (such as on signs, labels and comic strips). Give each child or pair of children a comic to search through and ask them to note any single word expletives (suggest that these are copied out in enlarged form and in their original print style to make a collective display).

When the children have got a good idea of a number of expletives, single word questions and so on, ask the class to work together to make a story which consists only of sentences of one word, for example: 'Look! Where? Here! Wow! Gosh! Gold! Hey! Stop! Thief!'

The children will come to realise that such stories depend on other words being implied and that the stories only make complete sense if they are illustrated (as a comic strip) or if they are acted out. Let them choose one form or other to complete the activity.

Follow-up
- Ask the children to write alternative multi-word sentences to go alongside their single word versions so as to make the stories explicit without illustration. The laboriousness of this could well demonstrate the succinct economy of the comic strip form.
- Let the children write, succinct three word stories using two nouns and a consequence.

Oh No!

Objective
To compose sequences of sentences for exclamatory effect.

Age range
Seven to eleven.

Group size
Any.

What you need
Paper, pencils.

What to do
Give the children an example of a personal strong reaction or over-reaction to a particular circumstance, for example: 'Oh no! What a day! The cat has been sick! It's raining yet again! The car wouldn't start! The goldfish jumped out of its bowl! My brother is in a mood! My work is a disaster! It's cold meat for dinner! Oh dear! Oh Dear! I simply can't believe it!'

Suggest that the children write out and elaborate on their own personal reactions to a particular circumstance, person or calamity. Write a number of possible starting lines on the board to help the children get started, for example:

- Disaster
- Stop!
- You so-and-so!
- What a surprise!
- Who would believe it! That is fantastic!
- Heavens!
- Wow!

Commands

At the double

Objectives
To focus on the fundamental grammatical process of word 'pivoting' – two-word sentence building.

Age range
Five to eight.

Group size
Any.

What you need
Paper, pencils.

What to do
Start by giving the children examples of two word commands which begin with the same word, for example: Look out! Look here! Look there! Look down! LOOK OUT! and so on.

Suggest or elicit some other words which lend themselves to 'pivoting' with further single words to make basic 'first' sentences: (Come... Sit... Stand... Go... Wait... Work... Don't... Stop... Please...).

Work with the children to make up some different peremptory commands beginning with these words. Point out that this is a process that very young children use when they first start talking: Mum Mum. Mum here. Mum Dinner. Mum sit! Mum chair! Mummmm!

After a few examples have been discussed and elaborated on, invite the children to compose and write out their own pivoting sequences or poems which they should try and finish with one particularly emphatic line.

Orders of the day

Objective
To practise making simple command sentences by citing and making fun of adult harassments.

Age range
Six to nine.

Group size
Any.

What you need
Experience of bossy adults or friends, if possible, a copy of the poem 'Chivvy' by Michael Rosen (in *You Tell Me*, Puffin Books), paper, pencils.

What to do
Discuss with the children the kind of things that bossy people say and situations where people tend to issue lots of commands. Read 'Chivvy' by Michael Rosen, if available. Ask the children to make up their own lists of bossy commands which they experience. As these are imperatives, they should each end with an exclamation mark; for example:

- Wake up!
- Get out of bed!
- Hurry up!
- Put on your clothes!
- Wash your face!
- Brush your teeth!
- Do up your shoes!
- Hurry hurry!

Statements

Captivating captions

Objective
To encourage the use and awareness of different grammatical structures in writing captions.

Age range
Five to eight.

Group size
Any.

What you need
Some large labels, finished pictures or models, felt-tipped pens.

What to do
Help the children to write captions for pictures or models that they have made by offering them particular grammatical formulas as frameworks to follow. There are a number of structures which particularly lend themselves to picture captions and which can also be composed readily in the 'sentence workshop' (see page 80). It is probably best to focus on just one or two for each occasion.

Here are a few such formulas:

- Elementary declarative sentences: 'This is a...' or 'Here is a ...'
- Exclamations: 'Look at this...' or 'Beware of tigers!'
- Questions: 'Who lives in this house?'
- Thoughts or speech: 'This grass is delicious,' said Daisy.
- Basic noun phrases: article + adjective(s) + noun (A big blue bag); article + adverb + adjective + noun; (An absolutely awful mess); article + noun + preposition... (A house with a big garden); article + noun + relative clause (The horse which ran the race); noun + action (Horses (which are) having a race).

Floating thoughts

Objective
To express spontaneous brief thoughts, each within a single sentence.

Age range
Six to eight.

Group size
Any.

What you need
Pieces of paper cut into bubble shapes, thread, adhesive, scissors, pencils, felt-tipped pens.

What to do
Talk with the children about how often odd ideas float into your head and then go away. Question some of them about what they are actually thinking at the moment or about odd ideas that have come to them recently. Prompt them with starting words like: 'I hope...', 'I wonder...', 'I can't wait until...', 'Wouldn't it be lovely if...'. 'I'm so hungry. I could eat a...' and so on.

Once the room is buzzing with thoughts, ask each child to write down one thought in a full sentence on a bubble-shaped piece of paper. Let them illustrate the thought on the reverse side of the paper. Check that each thought makes sense and is legible and then attach a piece of thread to hang them from the ceiling or a mobile frame but where the children can read them. Create a cloud of thoughts by grouping the bubbles together.

Follow-up
- Instead of directly drawing on their own thoughts, let the children imagine the thoughts of another character, say Father Christmas, a scarecrow, a fly on the wall or a pet.
- Invite the children to compose and make quantities of thought bubbles (even for inanimate objects) which they can superimpose on to pictures, either cut from magazines or ones they have drawn themselves.

Definitions

Objective
To practise and develop the art of making simple and eloquent defining sentences.

Age range
Six to eleven.

Group size
Any.

What you need
Paper, pencils, dictionaries, possibly an encyclopaedia.

What to do
Introduce the children to the principle of defining. You can approach this in a variety of worthwhile ways.

- Dictionary definitions – provide the children with a list of words which might be mutually confused (homophones, for example, would be particularly suitable) and ask the children to look them up in their dictionaries and then to say and/or write what the words mean. Explain that they must give a clear definition by writing the answer as full sentences. It could be prefaced something like this: Slug is a noun which denotes....
- Personal definitions – ask the children to: use similes for example, 'An apple is like a cricket ball but you can eat it'; use relative clauses for example, 'An apple is a fruit which is blown off trees'; use just adjectives and adverbs for example, 'An apple is round, quite small, red or green and delicious'.
- Broad definitions – provide a selection of concrete examples and ask the children to illustrate more abstract ideas (making metaphors, in effect) for example: Happiness is lying on a beach on a warm summer's day.

A is for apple
It is a round crisp fruit that grows on a tree.

It is like a cricket ball but you can eat it.

It is a fruit which can be put in pies.

It is a food that keeps the doctor away.

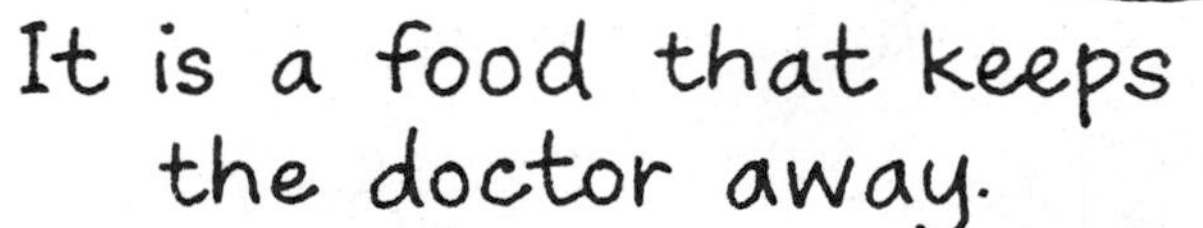

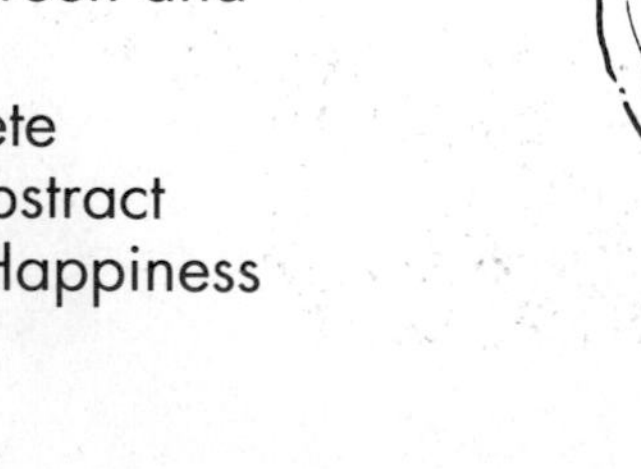

Who did what?

Objective
To make and/or write out a series of sentences which play upon a simple subject + predicate structure and which provide answers to who did what.

Age range
Six to nine.

Group size
Any.

What you need
An anthology of nursery rhymes, paper, pencils.

What to do
With the children, make a list of characters (subjects) associated with a particular setting, for instance, well-known nursery rhyme characters, characters of a particular book, film, television series, a collection of toys, a group of friends, animals in a zoo, inanimate objects in a room and so on. Ask the children to ascribe a different action to each subject to answer the question, 'what did they do?

Start composing a series of such sentences together – they could well be nonsensical. Let the children use the anthology to help them mix up nursery rhyme lines:

The cow went up the hill.
Jack jumped over the moon.
Jill lost her sheep.

Then ask the children to make their own lists of characters and actions, with a summary or 'twist' final sentence such as: They all went completely mad.

Idle thoughts

Objective
To make lists of random thoughts that arise in certain situations, such as, when lying in bed at night.

Age range
Seven to nine.

Group size
Any.

What you need
A quiet time, paper, pencils.

What to do
Introduce this writing activity without too much initial discussion as it draws upon personal semi-private reflection. Explain to the children that the idea is to try and capture (write down) random thoughts that come to mind on occasions when they are left on their own without much to do. Prompt them by suggesting one or two opening lines:
- When I lie in bed at night I think of....
- Round and round go the thoughts in my head.
- Sometimes I think of...

You could also offer them titles such as 'Just thinking', 'Wishing', 'Idle thoughts', 'Mixed thoughts', or 'Strange thoughts'. More interesting work should arise if you treat this as a relatively confidential exercise and assure the children that they will not necessarily have to share their thoughts with the rest of the class.

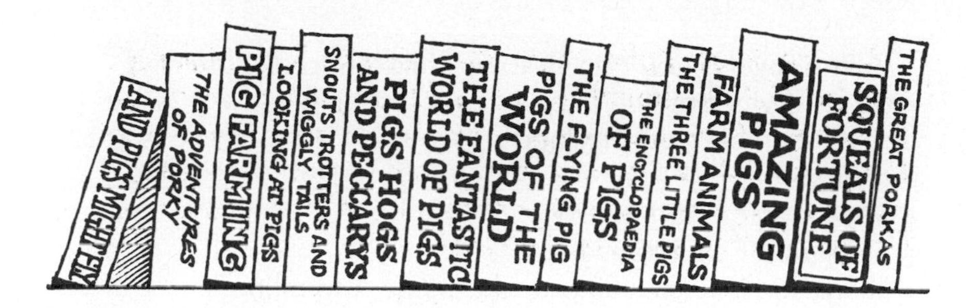

Fact and fancy

Objective
To practise making a series of simple declarative sentences either of fact or of fantasy.

Age range
Eight to ten.

Group size
Individuals or pairs.

What you need
A selection of information books, paper, pencils.

What to do
Allow the children, individually or in pairs, to choose an information book. Ask them to find out pieces of information which they didn't previously know or were not too sure about. Invite them to relate their new-found knowledge to the class, making sure that it is clearly expressed. Then suggest that they make up some fact sheets which follow a format something like this:

Do you know that...?

- A female pig is called a sow.
- A sow has a litter of up to 20 piglets at a time.
- Most pigs in this country live inside for all their lives.

Follow-up
Instead of making a list of true facts, ask the children to make a list of fanciful ideas:

Did you know that...?

- Pigs can fly.
- Sows can sing.
- Piglets like to dance.

Questions

Wondering why

Objective
To compose a series of 'why' or 'why not?' questions which may take a poetic form.

Age range
Six to ten.

Group size
Any.

What you need
Paper, pencils.

What to do
Decide whether to take this activity on one of two levels. With younger children, you may embark on a fairly long discussion followed by a general write up of genuine 'why' questions. For older children, a shorter discussion followed by a 'silent' reflective time is likely to be more rewarding.

Alternatively, you can ask the children to discuss and work on 'why don't ...?' questions, especially if the 'why don't?' is understood to mean, 'wouldn't it be fun if...?' For instance:

- Why don't chairs walk?
- Why don't sausages talk?
- Why don't daisies sing and cats go ting-a-ling?
- Why don't pigs fly?
- Why, oh, why, oh why?

Interviewing

Objective
To carry out personal interviews by preparing questions beginning with a range of interrogative words.

Age range
Seven to eleven.

Group size
Two or three children and then the whole class.

What you need
Photocopiable page 123, clipboards, paper, pencils, a chair, possibly a tape recorder.

What to do
Tell the class that they are going to practise doing some personal interviews to build up a picture of a person's interests, likes and dislikes, opinions, life history, plans, ambitions and general personality. Tell them that interviewees will be required but that first of all everybody has to prepare interview questions. To help them, give each child a copy of page 123. On this sheet there are a number of guidelines to help the children write at least two questions beginning with six different interrogative words.

Emphasise that the guidelines need not always be followed and that other lines of questioning are welcome. However, ensure that the children's questions are tactful and discreet.

When the interview questions have been prepared, ask a volunteer to answer questions about herself. The questions could be asked by particular interviewing panels (who have prepared their questions together) or by random selection from the rest of the class.

Follow-up
- Invite the children to adapt the questions for interviewing adult visitors or people outside the classroom.
- Make use of the interview information to write full personal profiles.

Raising questions

Objectives
To help and stimulate children to raise their own questions.

Age range
Six to eleven.

Group size
Any.

What you need
Small strips of paper, pencils.

What to do
Encourage the children to think up and raise questions about a topic before any general work is done. Challenge them to think about anything they might like to find out or know about the particular subject. Keep a record of all the questions; these could well form the basis of what work is done subsequently.

You can often obtain a more searching range of questions if, after a short discussion, you ask the children to write individual questions on slips of paper, putting down anything that occurs to them that they might like to know.

Help the children by writing some starter interrogative words on the board – Why...? When...? What...? Which...? Where...? How...? Who...? Do...? Accept good guesses for all other spellings so as not to inhibit ideas.

Sort out all the questions, edit them discreetly and make them into a composite question sheet. This can then form the basis of a more major project.

Testing out

Objective

To make questionnaire guides for vetting books, television programmes, foods and so on.

Age range

Eight to eleven.

Group size

Any.

What you need

Paper, pencils.

What to do

Discuss with the children the issue of personal taste including choices of books, favourite television programmes, foods and so on. Ask the children to suggest what questions they have in mind when choosing a book or perhaps when choosing a meal in a café. Tell the children that they are going to make a short questionnaire guide to help them make choices. Suggest that these could be entitled 'A book test', 'A friend test', 'A teacher Test', or 'A meal test'. Put a range of interrogative words on the board to help the children compile their questionnaires:

- Has it got plenty of good pictures?
- How many pages has it got?
- Is it fun to read or is it boring?
- Has it got anything about football?
- What does it smell like?
- Who is the author?

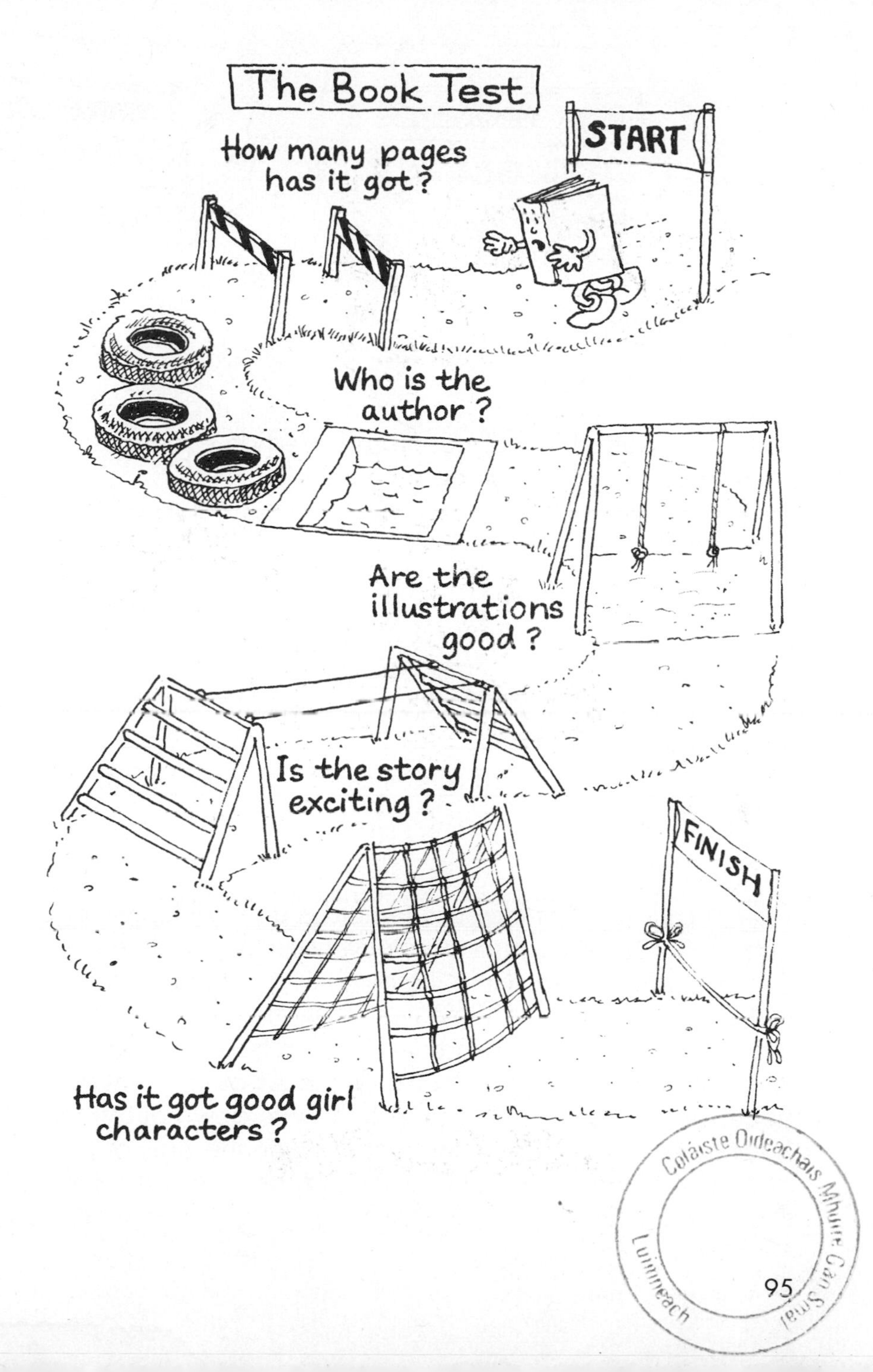

Quizzes

Objective
To make assorted lists of questions based on general knowledge in order to stage a quiz.

Age range
Seven to eleven.

Group size
Any.

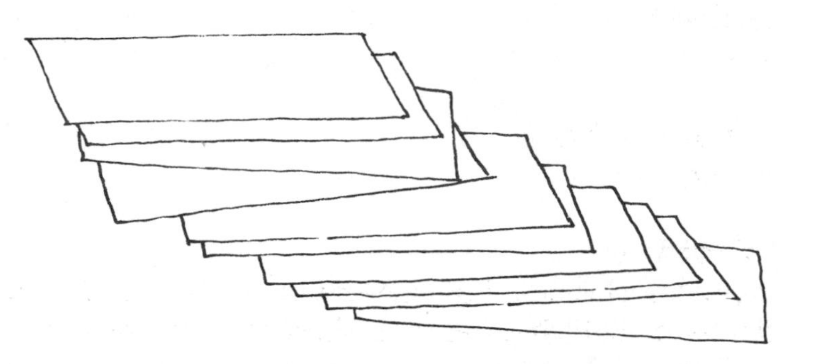

What you need
An encyclopaedia, good reference books, pencils, small slips of paper.

What to do
Tell the children that they are to hold a general knowledge quiz. This can be organised relatively quickly and efficiently if everybody contributes in the compiling of the questions. Distribute the encyclopaedias and reference books around the class and ask the children to browse through them until they come upon *relatively common* pieces of information about which they should devise and write down questions. Invite them to write down the questions on the slips of paper and to write the answer and also the reference source on the reverse side.

Explain to the children that they should select questions carefully so that the answers are not obvious but not too difficult. In other words, the question should be about something vaguely known by the child and confirmed in the book. Ask each child or small group of children to produce a small minimum number of questions. When you have a good collection of questions, let the children organise a quiz session.

Follow-up
Instead of a general quiz, ask the children to compile questions for a specialised one. This can be a good way of concluding a particular topic area or project and adding a test page to conclude a topic folder.

Explanations

Telling tales

Objective

To practise deliberately telling lies for story making.

Age range

Six to nine.

Group size

Any.

What you need

Paper, pencils.

What to do

If you tell children that they can make stories by just deliberately telling lies, this often helps to unblock creative inhibitions. A direct way of doing this is to ask the children to make a set number (say three or five) of lies about what they did last night, or a set number of lies about one of their parents, meeting a celebrity and so on. When the children have produced their lies, ask them to put them together to make a story along the following lines: 'Last night I made friends with a gang of robbers. We robbed a bank and put all the money in a sack'.

If and when

Objective

To prompt imaginative anticipatory thinking by deliberately introducing conditional and temporal sub clauses starting with 'if' or 'when'.

Age range
Seven to eleven.

Group size
Any.

What you need
Some good examples of poems and writings based on this idea (there are a good few in *Catapults and Kingfishers* by Pie Corbett and Brian Moses, Oxford University Press, paper, pencils.

What to do
Start by asking the children some 'what if' questions on the lines of, 'What would you do if you were prime minister/a teacher/a lion?'. Follow this by reading one or two poems based on this idea. Then ask the children to write some 'if' poems of their own. The formula framework to be followed could be written on the board – 'If I was... I would....

Suggest that all kinds of people, animals or inanimate objects can be substituted here. Options of power (such as being a prime minister, teacher, parent, ruler of the world, a lion or eagle, a fast car and so on) can be particularly appealing.

Follow-up
Ask the children to think and write about alternative beings and objects they might like to be:
- 'If I could be a wild animal I would be...';
- 'If I could be a toy I would be...'.

Let the children write speculations on an alternative world using starters like:
- 'If I was granted three wishes...';
- 'If chalk was cheese...';
- 'If pigs could fly...'.

Invite the children to write an autobiography through the stages of life:
- 'When I was born...';
- 'When I am very old...'.

Discuss and invite writing about different feelings and moods:
- 'If/when I am sad (lonely, happy, hungry, angry, fed up, bored, upset, tired, full of energy, feeling clever)...'.

Discuss and ask the children to write about what they like to do on a variety of different occasions.
- 'When the sun shines...';
- 'When it rains...';
- 'When Christmas comes...'.

Excuses excuses

Objectives
To provide an opportunity for generating sentences dealing with causation and reasoning, and to become familiar with the spelling of 'because'.

Age range
Seven to nine.

Group size
Any.

What you need
Pencils, paper.

What to do
Start this activity in a manner which will soon reveal itself to be slightly tongue in cheek, by picking on various members of the class for minor failings (or nonconformities) and demanding explanations:

- Why is your hair in a mess?
- Why do you keep on chattering?
- Why can't you sit still?
- Why were you late this morning?

Then go on to discuss with the children the idea of excuses. What are good excuses for various tricky occasions? When is it necessary to elaborate or to make excuses?

When no more excuses can be made for going on talking, ask the children to compose lists of excuses, or to write imaginary (or even genuine) letters of apology to a teacher or a parent. Suggest that the children follow particular models of sentence structure. For example:

- I am sorry I was late. It was because the cat was sick and the parrot kept on talking.
- I didn't finish my work because it was impossibly difficult.
- I only do it to annoy because I know it teases.

You might also suggest that the children make their excuses more and more preposterous. Invite them to conclude with a frank admission such as: 'It's all because, at heart, I just love being lazy'.

Follow-up
- Let the children make lists of explanations for everyday actions; for example: 'I get out of bed so that I can enjoy the day' and 'I brush my teeth in order to please my mum'.
- Discuss with the children the idea of chains of cause and effect and ask them to compose examples, maybe circular ones; for example: 'I go to school in order to learn, I learn so that eventually I can earn. I earn so that I can buy food...' and so on.

Reporting

Objective
To provide ideas and guidelines for effective reporting and relating of sequential events.

Age range
Seven to eleven.

Group size
Any.

What you need
A selection of newspapers reporting the same event or a selection of children's descriptions of one occasion, photocopiable page 124, paper, pencils.

What to do
Start with a general discussion about newspaper reports. Ask the children various questions such as:
- Who reads newspaper reports?
- Why do people write them?
- Why do reports of an event differ in different papers?
- Why are reports often a little exaggerated?
- What makes a report interesting?
- What do you want to find out if you read a report?

Steer the discussion to a consideration of the three main ingredients of any report:
- the opening or starting point (beginning);
- the sequence of what happened (middle);
- the conclusion and outcome of it all (end).

At this point, give each child a copy of 'the reporters guide' (photocopiable page 124) and explain it to them. Let the children use the guide as a framework for compiling several different kinds of report, such as:
- personal news stories in journals;
- accounts of a class outing;
- records of science activities or experiments;
- collections of news stories for a class newspaper.

Opening shots

Objective
To promote awareness of good opening sentences and so facilitate and stimulate them.

Age range
Seven to eleven.

Group size
Any.

What you need
A range of children's fiction books including some of the classics; paper, pencils.

What to do
Discuss with the children the problem and importance of starting any speech or piece of writing with a good opening line or sentence. Ask the children to look through a few fiction books and then invite them to read out a selection of opening sentences. Follow this by inviting them to make up their own opening sentences for stories, especially ones that make the reader want to know more.

Let the children write out their own first sentences, and some from good books and put them in a tray of story writing aids. Alternatively, they could write them on a poster and mount it on the classroom wall.

Story 'blurbs'

Objective
To compose three or four sentence story 'blurbs' which give enticing (but not complete) summaries of what stories are about.

Age range
Seven to eleven.

Group size
Any.

What you need
A few examples of story books with back-cover blurbs; some stories (written by the children or published ones) without blurbs; paper, pencils.

What to do
With the help of some examples, discuss with the children the purpose and composition of story 'blurbs'. Then invite them to try composing their own short blurbs for stories that have already been written. Give them these instructions to follow:

- Say and explain who the main character or characters are.
- Say when and where the story takes place.
- Give an idea of the principal course of events.
- Make a general hint about the nature of the outcome without giving away details or the actual denouement.

Follow-up
Encourage the children to use blurbs as story plans to help with the writing of the full story.

Getting the gist

Objective
To help pick out the key content words in a piece of text.

Age range
Eight to eleven.

Group size
Any.

What you need
Copies of text (such as articles from magazines and newspapers), coloured pencils or felt-tipped pens.

What to do
Explain and demonstrate to the children that they are going to use a quick and easy way to get the gist of a piece of writing. Show them how to do this by reading each sentence of a piece of text in turn, highlighting one or possibly two key words. After the children have been through the article, section of story or whatever, invite them to cut it out and mount the marked text. Suggest that they also add a banner headline of their own.

Punctuation and capitalisation

Punctuation and capitalisation are vital aspects of written language proficiency but they are not skills which can easily be separated out and specifically practised. All written sentence making implies a routine usage and recognition of particular punctuation and capitalisation signals. There's every reason to be punctilious about such practice. But that is more easily said than effectively done.

The activities in this section focus on editing processes and also the grasping of basic procedures and rules. There is less scope for creative experiment than in most of the other skill promotions.

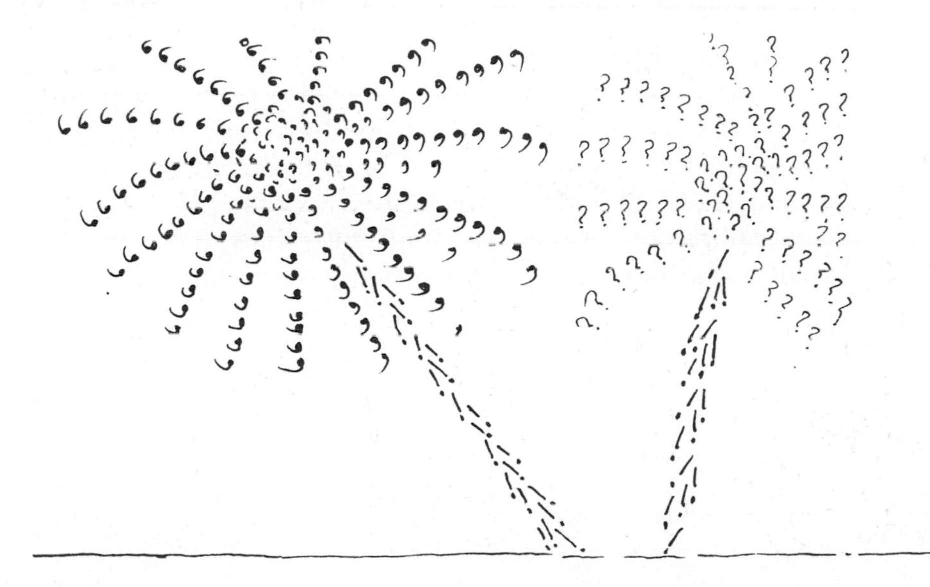

Punctuation fireworks

Objective
To become familiar with the forms of punctuation marks by using them to make patterned pictures.

Age range
Six to nine.

Group size
Any.

What you need
Dark grey drawing paper, coloured pencils.

What to do
Put various punctuation marks on the board and discuss with the children what they are usually used for. Show them that these marks can also be used for making patterns, especially firework patterns. Start by showing a simple exclamation mark which has several stops spraying out from it. Then show one or two other firework patterns based on ideas from the children.

When the children have an idea of the patterns that can be made, give each child a piece of paper and ask them to do some examples of their own, trying to use as many of the different punctuation marks as possible, and also using a range of colours.

Capital capitals

Objective
To make handwriting display squares which emphasise the forms and roles of capital letters.

Age range
Six to nine.

Group size
Individuals.

What you need
Unlined square pieces of writing paper (about 200mm x 200mm), scrap paper, pencils, coloured pencils, references of place and personal names (such as dictionaries and atlas indexes).

What to do
Tell the children that they are to create attractive squares using a particular capital letter. Demonstrate to them what they have to do and then let them do their own. Suggest that they choose a letter, possibly the initial letter of their first name or they could each be allotted a different letter of the alphabet.

Give each child a square of paper and ask them to fold it into four quarter squares and to rule three equally-spaced lines across the bottom two squares. Invite them to draw their chosen capital letter so that it fills the whole of the top left-hand square. Demonstrate how to decorate it like a traditional illuminated capital letter, possibly showing real examples in books. In the bottom of the top right-hand square, they should write out the remaining letters of the name but on a smaller scale to fill the line. Then on four horizontal lines across the bottom two squares, ask the children to write out various examples of their capital letter being used in appropriate contexts. For instance, on the first line there could be some other personal names; on the second line they could write some place names, and on the last two lines they could include two short sentences beginning with the same capital letter. It is probably best if the children practise on rough paper the words that they want to fill the bottom four lines. Allow the children to use dictionaries to help them choose their words.

Let younger children make simpler versions of this by drawing and decorating a decorated capital letter in each square.

Making the point

Objective
To demonstrate how spacing, punctuation and capitalisation helps to create written language and make it intelligible.

Age range
Six to eleven.

Group size
Any.

What you need
Photocopiable page 125, pencils, paper, a word processor (if possible).

What to do
Explain to the children that their task is to edit the piece of compressed script on photocopiable page 125 and add punctuation and so on. The neatest way of doing this is to use a word processor. However, if the children are to do it by hand, they should insert 'stroke' marks between the words before rewriting the text. Make the main editing task more specific by stating the number of full-stops, question marks, capital letters, and such like which are required for photocopiable page 125.

As a special challenge, ask some of the children to create unpunctuated pieces of text, copy them and ask the rest of the class to add the punctuation. Alternatively, you could use examples of stories written by members of another younger class and ask the children to punctuate the text.

Editing out 'and'

Objective
To edit long-winded narrative prose and over-long sentences into more manageable and eloquent forms.

Age range
Seven to ten.

Group size
Any.

What you need
Photocopiable page 126, Paper, pencils.

What to do
Tell the children that they are going to do some editing work, as is done in newspaper offices or by book publishers. Give each child a copy of photocopiable page 126. Ask them to read it and to comment on it, encouraging them to explain how easy or difficult it is to read. The children should conclude that the story has been written with too much urgency and needs to be made easier to read. In effect, it should be divided up into more manageable, shorter sentences with some of the over-repeated words (especially 'and') cut out or changed. To do this, explain that they will need to carry out editing procedures. The children can do this on two basic levels.

- Ask the children to make sure that not more than one 'and' is used in each sentence. Therefore, if there is a long sentence containing a whole string of clauses joined by 'and' they should edit out at least every other 'and' and put a stop in its place. They must then give each shortened sentence a new capital letter at the start. Suggest that one or two different words can be introduced to start these sentences. Ask the children to mark the old copy with a different colour. Finally, ask them to write out a new version of the story.
- Explain to the children that if the same subject is being used continuously, a series of main clauses can succeed each if they use commas to separate them all except the last two which can be joined by a conjunction. For example: 'Last night I had a row with my dad. I went out, slammed the door, jumped over the gate, ran down the road, raced round the corner and bumped straight into a big fat policeman'.

Let the children choose to do one or both types of edit. Display all the versions, including the original one, together to demonstrate the difference.

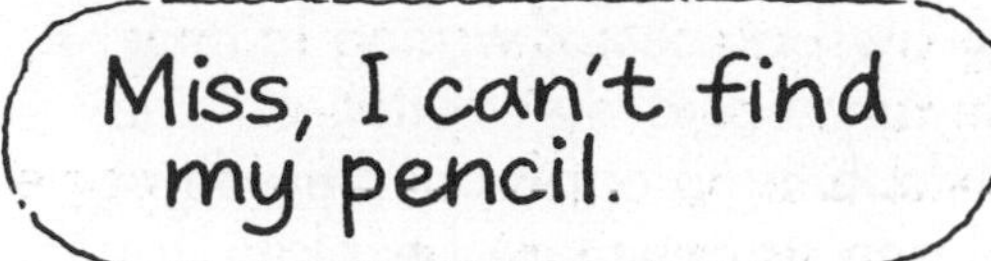

Snatching conversations

Objective
To capture everyday speech in writing with special attention to punctuation conventions.

Age range
Seven to eleven.

Group size
Small groups or the whole class, followed by individual work.

What you need
A tape recorder, paper, pencils.

What to do
Without any introduction, start writing on the board a comment or question which a child has just uttered in class, for example:

'Miss I can't find my pencil,' said David.

'Well,' said Miss Jones, 'you had better see if it has fallen on the floor.'

'Why are you writing all that on the board?' said David again.

'So that you can see how to write down snatches of talk,' said Miss Jones, 'and to make a kind of picture of what is happening in this room.'

- Demonstrate and encourage the children to use some variety in the placing of the spoken words, either at the beginning or end of sentences (or both). For instance:
David said, 'I can't find my rubber.'
'Miss,' said David, 'I can't find my book.'
'I can't find anything,' said David.
- Encourage alternatives to 'say' or 'said': muttered, asked, declared, whispered, replied, commented, shouted, shrieked and so on.

Use such an example as a basis for discussing and pointing out the punctuation conventions of using commas, inverted commas, and starting each new utterance on a new line. You can also point out how writing dialogue like this gives a vivid picture of what is going on – much more so than general descriptive statements.

When the children have appreciated the what, how and why of this, ask them to have a go at writing their own examples of conversation snatches using the punctuation conventions in a similar way to capture talk on their tables and around the class. Suggest that one or two small groups could try to do this by using a tape recorder and transcribing from a recording. They will probably find that this is a more laborious process.

Follow-up
- Playground calls, dinner time chat, adult gossip, kitchen talk, football commentary: ask the children to compose samples of talk that can be heard in a variety of other situations such as these.

Rounding up thoughts

Objectives
To round up, literally, the number of separate thoughts contained in continuous 'stream-of-consciousness' prose and to transcribe these into correctly capitalised and punctuated sentences.

Age range
Eight to eleven.

Group size
Any.

What you need
Paper, pencils, coloured pencils, a word processor (if possible).

What you do
Give the children a specified silent time (say up to 15 minutes) and ask them to write continually about anything that comes into their heads (or about anything they know and think about a specific subject). Explain that this is a kind of 'stream-of consciousness' writing exercise. The children will be encouraged if they see you doing this too.

Assure them that handwriting, spelling and punctuation do not matter, but rather, they should concentrate on the continuous transcribing of their thoughts. Ask them to try to make their writing relatively large and spacious.

When the time limit is reached, discuss how everyone felt about the activity. Ask the children to look at their writing again to see if they can count how many separate thoughts they wrote down. Show them from your example how they can ring and number each successive thought. Let them conclude this part of the exercise by adding titles like: 'Seventeen thoughts on a Tuesday morning.'

Later, quite possibly in a day or two's time, show the children how to edit their own pieces of writing in order to turn each thought into an appropriately capitalised and punctuated sentence. Invite them to carry out the editing with a different coloured pen or pencil and explain that this is standard practice carried out with all writing intended for publication. Point out that sometimes, two connecting thoughts might be joined into one sentence with a suitable conjunction. After careful editing, let the children rewrite the whole piece into a final draft form which would be acceptable for publication.

If you have access to a word processor, show the children how the editing procedure can be done on it.

Putting a stop to it

Objective
To draw attention to the three different sentence punctuation stops.

Age range
Eight to eleven.

Group size
Any.

What you need
Paper, pencils.

What to do
On the board write a short sentence like 'This is enough' three times once ending with an exclamation mark, once ending with a question mark and once ending with a full stop.

Ask the children to read these out loud using the appropriate intonations and discuss with them the importance of the final stop for indicating the kind of sentence as well as its boundary. Then ask and guide the children to compose a short series of remonstrating sentences which begin and end with exclamations and have a few questions and statements in between. For example:

- Enough is enough!
- Why do we always have to do writing?
- Why can't we sit back and enjoy ourselves?
- Why can't we just chat and tell jokes?
- I am tired of writing and writing and writing.
- I have done quite enough for today.
- Enough is enough!

Reproducible material

Beginning pairs, see page 15

a	a	a	a	e	e	e	e
e	e	e	i	i	i	i	o
o	o	o	u	u	u	b	b
c	c	d	d	f	f	g	g

Beginning pairs, see page 15

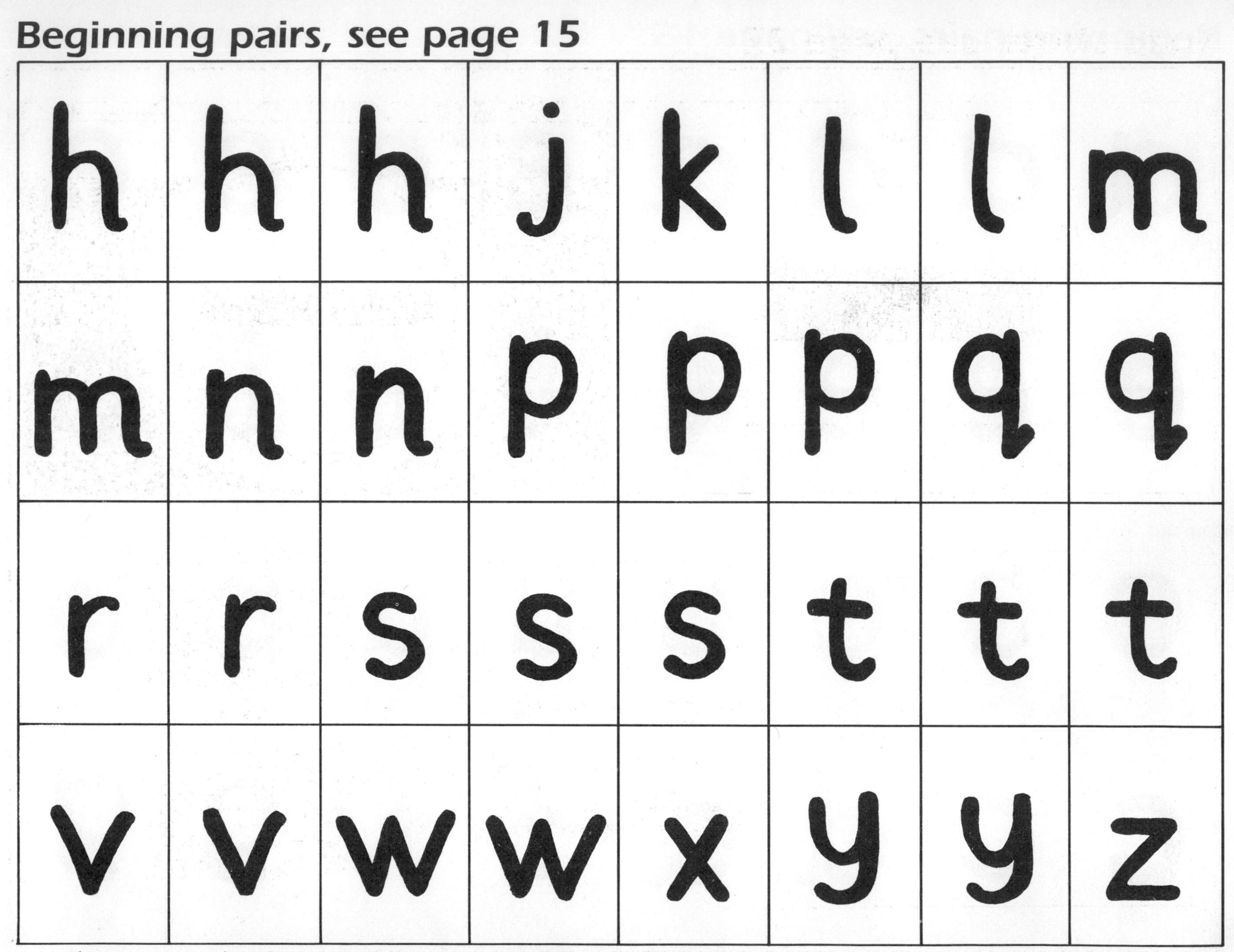

Snap shots, see page 27

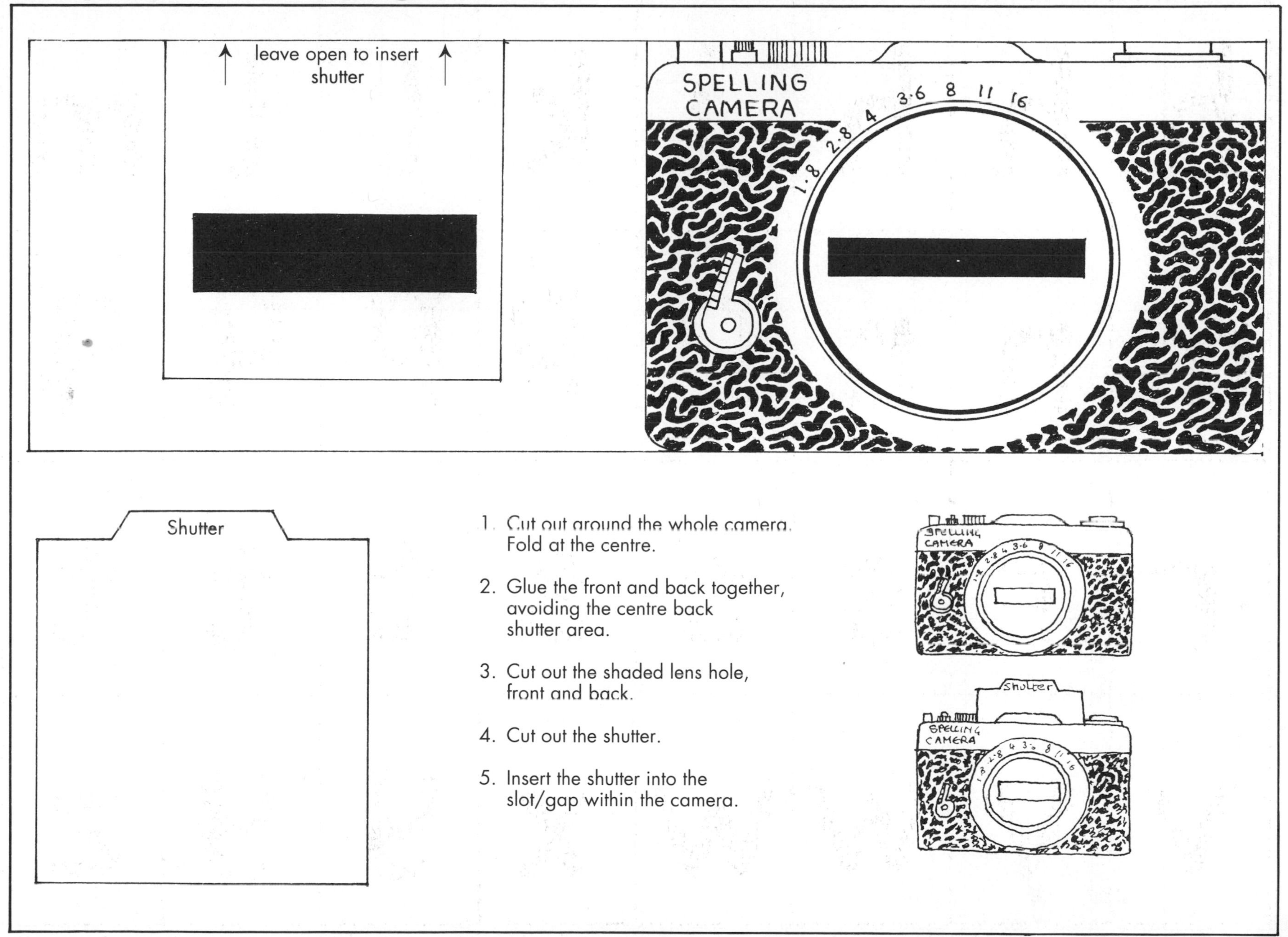

1. Cut out around the whole camera. Fold at the centre.
2. Glue the front and back together, avoiding the centre back shutter area.
3. Cut out the shaded lens hole, front and back.
4. Cut out the shutter.
5. Insert the shutter into the slot/gap within the camera.

Look! Write! Write! Write! Right! see page 29

① Spelling Processor
Look
and turn →

1.
2.
3.
4.
5.
6.
7.
8.

Fold under

② Write
and turn

1.
2.
3.
4.
5.
6.
7.
8.

③ Write again
and turn

1.
2.
3.
4.
5.
6.
7.
8.

① Fold under

④ and write again!

1.
2.
3.
4.
5.
6.
7.
8.

Fold over

⑤ Now open and check →

Are these the same? ?

1. ✓ or X
2. ✓ or X
3. ✓ or X
4. ✓ or X
5. ✓ or X
6. ✓ or X
7. ✓ or X
8. ✓ or X

Which witch is which? see page 30

HOMOPHONES

arc (curve) **ark** (boat)
beach (seashore) **beech** (tree)
bean (plant or kind of seed) **been** (has been)
blue (colour) **blew** (blowing)
bough (branch) **bow** (bend)
chute (a slide) **shoot** (fire at)
deer (animal) **dear** (expensive)
die (lose life) **dye** (colour)
eight (8) **ate** (have eaten)
fort (castle) **fought** (fighting)
great (big) **grate** (fireplace)
hare (animal) **hair** (on head)
heel (of foot) **heal** (cure)
higher (taller) **hire** (rent)
hoarse (husky) **horse** (animal)
it's (it is) **its** (belonging to it)
Jim (James) **gym** (gymnastics)
knew (know) **new** (just made)
leant (leaned) **lent** (borrowed)
lock (fasten) **loch** (Scottish lake)
made (making) **maid** (girl)
meat (flesh) **meet** (join)
muscle (of body) **mussel** (shellfish)
not (no) **knot** (tied string)

oar (for rowing) **ore** (mineral) **or** (alternately)
pain (suffering) **pane** (window)
pair (two) **pear** (fruit)
peace (quiet) **piece** (a part)
peer (stare or lord) **pier** (jetty)
place (position) **plaice** (fish)
queue (a line of people) **cue** (hint or billiard-stick)
rain (water drops) **reign** (rule)
sail (or a ship) **sale** (selling)
slay (kill) **sleigh** (sledge)
sure (certain) **shore** (beach)
tale (story) **tail** (end)
there (place) **their** (belonging to them)
to (towards) **too** (also or too many) **two** (2)
urn (pot) **earn** (make pots of money)
vain (proud) **vane** (weathercock) **vein** (blood vessel)
week (seven days) **weak** (not strong)
weather (rain or sunshine) **whether** (if)
which (what) **witch** (woman)
whole (all) **hole** (hollow)
won (winning) **one** (single)
you (person) **ewe** (female sheep) **u** (letter)

THE TROUBLE WITH SPELLING

Spelling is such a funny business. In the England language there are thousands upon thousands of words. They come in all kinds of letter arrangements, meanings, shapes and sizes. Some are beautiful, some are ugly, some are easy to recognise, others can be confusing to distinguish or else fiendishly difficult to remember. Just look at these words:

curious, cough, coffee, tough, thought, through, mischief, naughtiness, beauty, photograph, oceans, lotions, lieutenants, sugar, sausages, shoes, who, how, know and NO!

Why do so many of our words have such funny and difficult spellings? Couldn't they be made in a more sensible way? That is what some people argue. They want English spellings to be changed so that they all follow easy rules and so become *eesyur to lurn* (or so they believe). What do you think?

Another puzzling question about spelling is this:

Why do some people find spelling easy to learn while other people have a lot of trouble?

Being clever does not necessarily help you to be a good speller. The great scientist Albert Einstein and the famous writer William Shakespeare were both known to be poor spellers. So was the American president George Washington. Another American president, Andrew Jackson, said, 'It's a damned poor mind that can think of only one way to spell a word.' So, if you are having a problem or two/to/too with spelling yourself, take heart! You are in good company.

But there is one thing we can all do for now. We can look out for the hard spots – the nasty, difficult bits that often catch us out, like in these words:

Christmas, scratch, exciting, bicycle, ceiling, action.

Can you spot any others which are tricky for you on this page?

Cloze procedure, see page 36

WORDS AT WORK

Watch out for words! They can do ______________ tricks. They are ______________ ______________ invention.

Words can give name labels to thinks like, for instance, ______________, ______________, ______________ or ______________.

Some kinds of words can describe how the things look, saying whether they are ______________, ______________, ______________ or ______________. Words like this are known as ______________.

Other kinds of words can say what things can do, if they can ______________, ______________, ______________ or ______________.

These special words are ______________. They sometimes have other words to go with them to say how or when things happen or are done, maybe ______________ly, ______________ly or ______________. These one are known as ______________.

What is more, there are even words which can tell where anything is and where things happen. This may be ______________ a house, ______________ a roof, ______________ a chimney, ______________ the road, ______________ a bridge, ______________ the sky or just anywhere. Guess what these are called! ______________!

So watch out for ______________ words and all their ______________ tricks. They can make noises or else they sit ______________ on a page. They work in ______________ ______________ ways.

Embroidering, see page 58

Once there was a girl. She lived in a house. She lived with her mother, brothers, cat, dogs and goldfish. She had friends. She was happy.

One day she went out with her brothers and dogs for a walk. They went along the road, across the park and into the forest. They walked and walked for a way until they became tired. They sat down for a rest. Soon they all fell asleep. When they woke up it was dark. They were hungry, cold, frightened and they couldn't see a thing.

Then there was a noise What was it?

Action stations, see page 64

Watch television.	Drive the car.	Run in the park.	Feed the cat.	Tell a joke.	Stay in bed.	Climb a tree.	Lick an ice-cream cone.
Go shopping.	Eat breakfast.	Catch the bus.	Walk the dog.	Wash up.	Tidy my room.	Get ready for school.	Play hide and seek.

Absolutely amazing reviews, see page 70

REVIEWING GUIDE WORDS

Adverbs

amazingly staggeringly incredibly
terrifically hysterically uproarously
blisteringly absolutely extraordinarily
tremendously hugely extremely
supremely ever so very not not at all
quite mostly slightly just never
only almost hardly occasionally
unusually strangely totally partly
scarcely
_____ly _____ly _____ly _____ly

Adjectives

excellent beautiful brilliant wonderful
exciting thrilling spell-binding terrifying
awful frightening frightful rude
enjoyable pleasurable happy stunning
surprising entertaining soppy skilful
delightful enjoyable super superb
outstanding terrible appalling disgusting
shocking successful clever fascinating
funny amusing disappointing pathetic
informative interesting dull boring
ghastly _______ _______ _______
_______ _______ _______ _______

Positioning words, see page 72

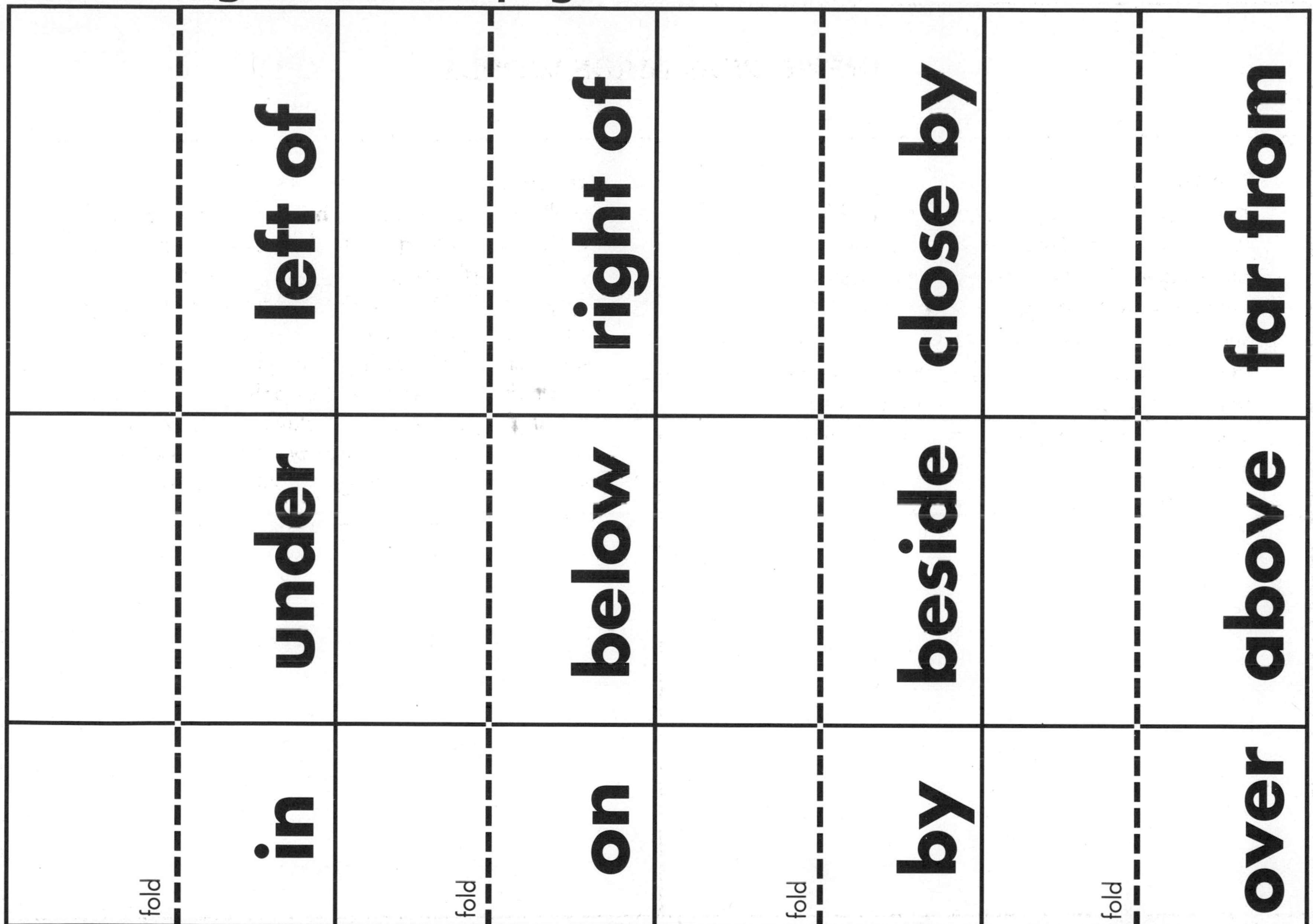

The sentence workshop, see page 80

look	looked	cats	I	old	very	the
take	took	dogs	you	red	always	a
sit	sat	girls	me	good	never	an
come	came	boys	she	green	slowly	some
eat	ate	apples	he	huge	usually	any
are	were	elephants	they	pretty	not	or
think	thought	dragons	them	ugly	fast	and
run	ran	houses	it	little	suddenly	but

Interviewing, see page 93

	Questions	Answers
Who? (favourite sportsperson, author, TV or pop star, best friends, oldest friend ....)		
What? (favourite food, colour, animal, day, lesson, TV programme, book, shop....)		
When? (get up, go to bed, favourite time of day of year, birthday....)		
Where? (live, like to play, go at weekends or on holiday, favourite place....)		
How? (come to school, old are you, old is your house, how many family pets, do you feel.... ?)		
Why? (following any answer from the above, go to school, explain behaviour and personal habits....)		

A REPORTER'S GUIDE

What was the event or occasion?

___

1. The beginning

The place ___

The time ___

Who was there? ___

Any special circumstances (to do with the weather, feelings or other things happening) ___

___

What started the story? ___

___

2. The sequence of events

(1) ___

___

(2) ___

___

(3) ___

___

3. The conclusion

The final action

___

The final state of affairs

___

A general opinion about the whole story and its significance

___

Suggestion for a title

___

Making the point, see page 105

WHAT'S THE POINT OF PUNCTUATION?

here is some writing without any punctuation you will see that there
are no full stops no commas and no question or exclamation marks
there are no signs anywhere to tell you where to pause or to take a
breath you will see that this kind of writing is quite difficult to read
what a nuisance it is can you make sense of it easily or do you have
to puzzle over it more than you usually do with normal writing are
you beginning to appreciate what a brilliant invention punctuation is
with just a few tiny marks you can do magic to your writing and
make it so much more fun for everybody in this passage you will see
that there are actually twelve sentences which need to be signalled
with twelve new capital letters seven full stops three question marks
and two exclamation marks there should also be four or five commas
can you now try to put these marks in their place good luck

sometimespeoplewritewithoutpunctuationandwithoutleavinganyspace
betweenwordsthisisparticularlytroublesomeforanybodywhotriestoread
itisntitbutitwillbenotroubleforycutosortoutwillit

Editing out 'and', see page 106

A STORY FOR EDITING

Last night I had a row with my dad and I
went out and slammed the door and jumped
over the garden gate and then I ran down the
road and I raced round the corner and I
bumped straight into a big fat policeman
and he tried to hold on to me but I ran
off and disappeared and then I found my
friends and I told them I was on the run
and they said we should all go up to the
playing field so we did and we had a
brilliant game of football and I scored
two goals and then who should we see
coming across the field but that policeman
but I don't think he saw me and I was
not taking any chances so I went off with
my friends round to the side entrance
and ran through the back street all the
way home and my dad went absolutely
mad at me

Some other words which might start some of the sentences:

Afterwards Next Straightaway
Soon Later So Finally

Index of skills

adjectives 24, 34, 54–60, 70, 79, 90
adverbs 34–36, 67–71, 79, 84, 88
alliteration 11, 54, 104
alphabetical order 12, 44, 46, 47, 54
anagrams 42
articles 34–36, 61, 79

beginnings 9, 15, 101

capitals 38, 40–43, 104
captions 39, 86
causal clauses 99
cloze procedure 36
compound words 21
comprehension 101–102
conditional clauses 98
conjunctions 34–36, 76–77, 106
consonants 14, 17, 31
contractions 53, 88

declarative sentences 50, 86–91, 109
definitions 10, 51, 61, 88
demonstration 50
dictionary use 10, 15, 18, 25, 34, 47, 54, 59, 88
direction (*see* letter directions or prepositions)

editing 57, 105–106, 108
exclamations 82–83, 86, 109
explanatory sentences 97–102

fiction 91, 97

handwriting technique 11, 16, 22, 23, 29, 76, 94
headlines 10, 70, 100, 102
homophones 30, 88
hyperbole 57, 69, 70

imperatives 84–85
indexes 44, 46
information processing 44, 91, 93, 96, 100, 101, 102
initial letters 11, 12, 14, 15, 18, 104
interjections 9, 34–35, 79, 82–83
interrogatives 93–96
interviews 93

labels 8, 37–38, 55
letter directions 16, 22
letter formation 11, 16, 22, 104
letter sequences 14, 15, 18, 22, 23, 25
lists 8, 10, 43–45, 47, 54

metaphors 88

nouns 20, 21, 24, 34–46, 65, 79

plurals 20, 40, 65
poetic language 11, 45, 56, 66, 73, 98, 109

prefixes 22, 25
prepositions 25, 34–36, 72–75, 79
pronouns 34–36, 48–52, 79, 88
proper nouns 38, 40–43, 104
punctuation/marks 76–77, 103, 105–109
puzzles 42, 49, 51, 56

questions 30, 73, 92–96, 109
quizzes 96

relative clauses 57, 88
reports 100
reversals 16

similes 57, 60, 69, 88
speech 82, 107
spelling anomalies 10, 11, 28, 30–31
spelling technique 19, 27–29, 31
stories 77, 97, 100, 101, 106
substitution 14, 79
syllables 26
synonyms 47, 59

tenses 62, 65
thoughts 87, 90, 108

verbs 23, 34–36, 62–66, 79, 83–85
vowels 12, 17, 31

References

Catapults and Kingfishers – Teaching Poetry in Primary Schools, Pie Corbett and Brian Moses (Oxford University Press).

Children's Writing in the Primary School, R. Beard (Hodder and Stoughton).

The Emergence of Literacy, Nigel Hall (UKRA/Hodder and Stoughton).

English in the National Curriculum, Department of Education and Science (HMSO).

Guides to Good English: Good Spelling, Good Words, Good Grammar, Good Writing, W. Edmonds (Kingfisher).

Problem Solving in Primary Schools (ed.) Robert Fisher (Blackwell).

The Puffin Book of Spelling Puzzles, W. Edmonds (Penguin).

The Quality of Writing, Andrew Wilkinson (Oxford University Press).

Spel... is a Four-Letter Word, Richard Gentry (Scolastic).

Spelling Caught or Taught, M. Peters (Routledge).

Writing: Teachers and Children at Work, D. Graves (Heinemann).

Writing and the Writer, Frank Smith (Heinemann).

The Writing of Writing (ed.) Andrew Wilkinson (Oxford University Press).